JOHN WAYNE'S WAY

CODE OF THE WEST: From his earliest B Westerns—even in the advertising posters employed to fire a potential audience's imagination—John Wayne always captured the highest values of an American hero. *Courtesy: mptvimages.com*

JOHN WAYNE'S WAY

LIFE LESSONS
FROM THE DUKE

DOUGLAS BRODE

TWODOT®

GUILFORD, CONNECTICUT
HELENA, MONTANA
AN IMPRINT OF ROWMAN & LITTLEFIELD

A · T W O D O T® · B O O K

An imprint of Rowman & Littlefield

Distributed by NATIONAL BOOK NETWORK

Copyright © 2014 by Douglas Brode

TwoDot is a registered trademark of Rowman & Littlefield.

British Library Cataloguing-in-Publication Information available

Library of Congress Cataloging-in-Publication Data available

ISBN 978-0-7627-9629-8

∞™ The paper used in this publication meets the minimum requirements of American National Standard for Information Sciences—Permanence of Paper for Printed Library Materials, ANSI/NISO Z39.48-1992.

TO MY SON SHANE, WHO GREW UP AS STRONG
AND STRAIGHT AS HIS NAMESAKE

CONTENTS

EVERYTHING I NEED TO KNOW I LEARNED FROM WATCHING JOHN WAYNE MOVIES

Here's a story that Maureen O'Hara, John Wayne's all-time favorite female co-star, loved to share with the press and/or public when asked about the Big Guy, all six feet four inches of him. One night, as the two went for a drive, they talked and talked, as old friends love to do. After a while the Duke, who was behind the wheel, decided he could use a drink. Problem was, they were now passing through a suburban area. No bars in sight, only one pleasant house after another. The situation frustrated Wayne. Never one to sit back and let a problem—any problem—eat away at him, Duke took the initiative, even as one of his glorious on-screen characters might do.

In this case he slowed down and pulled over to the side of the street, then randomly picked one of the homes in which living room lights were still on and visible through the front windows. Wayne opened the passenger door for a stunned O'Hara and walked her to the entrance, where he unhesitatingly rang the buzzer. Shortly, a middle-aged fellow cracked open the door. Only half believing what he saw, the man tried to form words, but could not.

"Hello," Wayne said, nodding his head with the same gallantry his Col. David Crockett employs when meeting fictional Flacca (Linda Cristal) for the first time in *The Alamo*. "John Wayne. And Maureen O'Hara! We were passing by, in the mood for a drink. We wondered if perhaps you might be serving alcohol tonight, and willing to invite a few uninvited guests?"

"Of course, Mr. Wayne," the gentleman stammered.

"*Duke*," Wayne insisted, shaking the fellow's hand, inquiring as to who he might be.

For the next several hours, Wayne and O'Hara enjoyed drinks and conversation. The one thing Duke didn't want to talk about was himself, which in itself sets him apart from most Hollywood types. He wanted to know all about these people. Who were they? How did they meet? What faraway lands did their families once call home? What did this guy do for a living? Wayne's interest was sincere. After all, these were those very people who, for decades, had supported him and his own family, thanks to ticket sales at their local bijou. And unlike some full-of-themselves stars, Wayne never for a moment forgot that his career was entirely at their mercy, his yearly status as one of the world's top ten box office stars a result of their unflagging support.

Wayne relished the opportunity to deal with the folks not as a mass (how he, quick to anger at the sight of the color red owing to its modern political implications, hated that word!), but as *individuals*. Not "the crowd." *Never* the crowd, but as people who, when they do on occasion come together, constitute the American community, hardly an unimportant entity. First and foremost for Wayne, though, they were individuals. So it was best to get to know them one-on-one, face-to-face. A century and a half earlier, Davy Crockett (1786–1836) had understood that. So too did the man who incarnated that American hero on the big screen.

Whether that story happens to be historical or only a myth (more likely a legend, somewhere between the extremes) matters less than how perfectly it fits the Duke, on-screen or off. John Wayne, man of action. A cowboy or contemporary warrior. Sailor or flyer. The fellow who lived out our wildest, most wondrous dreams of adventure, while illustrating time after time the manner in which one strong, righteous individual truly could make a difference in a jaded world on the brink of ruin.

Also, O'Hara's fable defines Wayne as he has come down to us today, an icon of what it means to be an American: brash, friendly, supremely self-aware; willing to try pretty much anything, just to see if it flies. That was and, thanks to the immortality of celluloid, remains the John Wayne of that long-ago L.A. night. The persona called John Wayne and the person born Marion Morrison were, mostly, inseparable. In everyday life John Wayne viewed problems, large and small, as so many hurdles that had to—and, most importantly, *could!*—be overcome.

The larger point is this: Even those who haven't heard that tidbit of a tale can relate to the ways in which Wayne handled whatever came his way, because there are the films, some 250 of them. They range from his early low-budget juvenile oaters to *Red River, The Searchers, Rio Bravo,* and several others that rate among the greatest Westerns ever made. Then again, not all were cowboy movies. The Duke could play light comedy with the best of them. He even once took a turn at serious human drama by no less than Eugene O'Neill, America's answer to William Shakespeare. As you read through the film synopses in this book, you can't help but notice how often Wayne's characters are called "John" or "Duke," that nickname acquired from an adopted dog during his boyhood. More often than not, the image on-screen—whatever his name happens to be this time around—is, we all know, Wayne himself.

In most cases Wayne on-screen proffered a role model. Even when Duke played a dastardly character, as in *Reap the Wild Wind* or *Wake of the Red Witch*—a pair of monstrous captains equal to Nordhoff and Hall's fact-based Bligh or Jack London's quasi-fictional Sea Wolf—he did so in a manner that, without need for didacticism,

BEYOND POLITICS: Let us all take a lesson from John Wayne and Barbra Streisand who, on Oscar night 1970, put aside the terrible strains that threatened to tear our country apart, expressing their mutual admiration as people and talents—proving that now, as in the past, if Americans do not all hang together, we surely will all hang separately. *Courtesy: mptvimages*

informed us via a cautionary fable. Such characters' ignominious deaths remind the audience that the yarns provide the yellow traffic lights of life itself, while their deep flaws represent examples of what we as viewers would be wise to avoid.

First and foremost, of course, he set out to entertain. A free-market capitalist to the very core, Duke understood the importance of paying back the ticket buyer with a good time out at the movies. But such diversion did not preclude saying something serious along the way. And for those of us who devotedly went to see every John Wayne film on release, likewise catching up with the earlier ones on their TV reruns and now DVD, we've always been at least somewhat aware that these are in truth pieces of a great jigsaw puzzle. Put them together, and you learn something. Let's call it Wayne's "Way": a means of dealing with life, from the ordinary to the extreme situations each of us sooner or later faces.

Here's an example of that problem solving from Wayne's reality that reasserts how similar his movie persona and actual person were. Back in the late 1970s, even as the presidency of Democrat Jimmy Carter neared its end, Wayne was among the first to announce his upcoming support for friend (and one-time fellow cowboy star) Ronald Reagan as the Republican presidential contender. Meanwhile, the Republicans in Congress were in the process of giving Carter a hard time on any issue that arose, with little consideration as to the right and/or wrong involved in any such legislation. At that time Carter announced that he intended to return control of the Panama Canal to its home nation, a promise that had been made by previous presidents, including Republicans. Here was grist for the mill of all-out attack. If Carter favored this, then by God they were against it, and they would fight the sitting president every inch of the way.

ONCE IS NOT ENOUGH: Wayne so enjoyed playing Rooster Cogburn in *True Grit* that he essayed the role a second time in the eponymously titled sequel. *Courtesy: mptvimages.com*

That's when the Duke entered the picture. He contacted President Carter and promised his full support, then reached out to every one of the Republicans snapping around Carter on this situation. In a polite but firm manner, Wayne let them know the wisdom of backing off on this issue. Yes, conservative Republican Wayne disagreed with liberal Democrat Carter on most policies. But not on this one, which cut across political lines. "There's right and there's wrong," as Duke's Davy Crockett announces in *The Alamo*, and which Wayne demonstrated not only in movies, but in life as well. Lest we forget, as Aristotle declared more than two thousand years ago, art is always an imitation of life. And today, art includes movies (at least the best of them).

Thanks to John Wayne, control of the Panama Canal was indeed properly handed over to its own people. Carter never forgot this beau geste. Wayne had meant precisely what he said when attending Carter's inaugural ball even though he'd campaigned for Gerald Ford: "I'm the loyal opposition—with the emphasis on loyal." A decade and a half earlier, when Wayne's candidate Richard Nixon lost the election to John F. Kennedy and the Duke was asked for a reaction, he said: "He was not my candidate. He is now my president. I wish him only the best."

There are many other biographical bits involving John Wayne from which each of us could learn, particularly in the unnecessarily heated world of today's divided America. Wayne's own love of country always emphasized what we have in common, not the differences that, if we allow them to, can drive us apart. Far more fun, though, is watching Wayne the actor. Each of his movies has at least one key line that expresses not only the writer or director, but the star. After all, at their best, movies offer not merely an escape from reality, but a means of comprehending it.

AN INAUSPICIOUS DEBUT: Though Duke had played bit parts in a handful of motion pictures, including several for John Ford, his first lead was in an ill-fated attempt to create the initial talkie Western-epic. *Courtesy: mptvimages.com*

THE BIG TRAIL (1930)

Director: Raoul Walsh and Louis R. Loeffler
Screenwriters: Marie Boyle, Jack Peabody, Florence Postal, and Fred
Sersen (screenplay based on a story by Hal G. Evarts)
"No great trail was ever built without hardship."

In his first lead role, as Breck Coleman, a twenty-three-year-old Wayne
utters those words as part of a grand inspirational speech to pilgrims
traveling west via covered wagon train to Oregon. They have suffered
drought on the desert, brush fires on the prairie, sudden Indian attacks,
and seemingly insurmountable mountains. Finally they are trapped
in a raging blizzard. Exhausted, their initial ambitions withered, this
American community is ready to give up. That's when the rugged individualist who has been serving as trail guide delivers a rousing oration
worthy of England's Henry V (or at least Shakespeare's incarnation
of him) at Agincourt. "When you stop fighting," Breck insists, "that's
death." This is about more than themselves. Whether they know it or
not, this group represents the spirit of the American West that inspires
countless others and becomes embedded in our nation's history . . .
as embodied by this very film. Prodded on by Coleman's exhortation,
"We got to suffer!" the pioneers somehow get going again and reach
their destination. Though this epic proved a box office failure, causing
the then little known Wayne (Walsh originally wanted Gary Cooper)
to drift into B movies for the better part of a decade, the persona that
would define the Duke for all time had here been set in cement.

*THE MESSAGES: (1) No pain, no gain; (2) never, ever, ever quit; and
(3) if you keeping telling yourself, "I refuse to fail," you WILL succeed—
in God's good time, though, not your own.*

THE HURRICANE EXPRESS (1932)

Directors: Armand Schaefer and J. P. McGowan
Screenwriters: Colbert Clark, Barney Sarecky, Wyndham Gittens, George Morgan, and J. P. McGowan
"Too bad she's out of date."

If you really want to grasp how down-and-out Duke was after the box office failure of *The Big Trail*, get this: Though he had the lead in this twelve-episode Mascot Pictures serial, Wayne didn't receive top billing. That went to several character people who populate this romance-of-the-rails drama. In the opening Wayne's protagonist, Larry Baker, a young pilot, visits his dad (J. Farrell MacDonald), who has spent his life working on the railroad, with most of that time dedicated to the engine that lends the film its title. Aware of the machine's reliability and beauty, Baker nonetheless smiles and says the above words. When his dad is killed shortly thereafter by a saboteur known only as "the Wrecker," Baker sets out to learn the true identity of that villain, as well as unmask a vast conspiracy that is trying to destroy the old-fashioned train company. Although the grieving son accomplishes his mission—with the help of a most courageous female lead (Shirley Grey)—while fighting his way through the shadowy forces of evil, he comes to regret his initial glib statement. The realization finally dawns on him that there is room for both the new idea of flying and the old yet still important means of travel from the previous century.

THE MESSAGE: Only fools opt for extremism, insisting on old over new or vice versa. Wise men know to appreciate the traditional, yet be open to what's best in our emerging world.

A CONTEMPORARY COWBOY: Though Wayne is here cast as a modern man in a suit, the romance, adventure, and threatening situations associated with Westerns were updated for an excitingly relevant thriller.
Courtesy: Mascot

THE ODD COUPLE: For this edge-of-your-seat contemporary cliffhanger, the Big Guy teamed with diminutive "Little Billy" Rhodes, the latter a full partner in their mission to bring bad guys to justice.   *Courtesy: Mascot*

THE SHADOW OF THE EAGLE (1932)

Directors: Ford Beebe and B. Reeves Eason
Screenwriters: Ford Beebe, Colbert Clark, and Wyndham Gittens
"Your eyes gave you away."

Here's another cliffhanger, with Duke once more playing a young flyer. Lest we forget, daredevil pilots were, during the early twentieth century, an airborne equivalent of the cowboy heroes of the nineteenth century, so it makes perfect sense young Wayne played his fair share of both. Here he's Craig McCoy, attached to a sad little carnival show that survives from day to day by playing small towns that are bereft of any other entertainment. The old owner (Edward Hearn) is wheelchair bound, so his plucky go-getter daughter, Jean (Dorothy Gulliver), must run the show. When her dad is kidnapped (or so it seems), Jean must simultaneously save the day while trying to figure out some mysterious skywriting by a cryptic figure known only as "the Eagle." Even this strong Lois Lane type needs help, and her Superman is the Duke. This movie offers some great humor as McCoy runs around foiling criminals with Wayne's most unlikely sidekick ever: "Little Billy" Rhodes as the carnival's sideshow midget. By the final chapter all the loose ends have been wrapped up, and Craig explains how he figured out the nature of the crimes. In the quote above he also reveals how he deduced that Jean loves him and him alone.

THE MESSAGE: You can learn a lot about people by listening closely to what they say—and sometimes more by noticing what their eyes say.

THE TELEGRAPH TRAIL (1933)

Director: Tenny Wright
Screenwriter: Kurt Kempler
"No man can stop the progress of the West."

This B picture was one of several Wayne made for Warner Bros./ Vitagraph Pictures before he sank into shoestring budgets over at Poverty Row (Hollywood's nickname for the on-the-edge-of-respectability area where smaller studios churned out junk movies were located). This short tale of the coming of the telegraph cleverly integrated impressive stock-footage action sequences into the narrative for a mini-epic impact. Duke plays John Trent, an army scout assigned to keep the communications lines open. (Incidentally, the steed Wayne rode during the movie—one of Hollywood's famous Wonder Horses—also was named Duke. The two appeared together in several projects.) The baddie here is a reactionary named Lynch (Albert J. Smith) who's been gouging the locals with high-priced goods his men bring in on freighters. The reason only he can get his supplies through Indian territory is that he's struck a deal with Chief High Wolf (Yakima Canutt). Though "red devils" and other such now verboten slurs do appear here, it's important to note that the true villains are not those native people desperately defending their homeland, but this capitalist of the rawest sort who thinks only about profits, leading to a great loss of life on both sides. When Trent speaks the above line, he's referring to Lynch, not High Wolf.

THE MESSAGE: Although it's important to respect traditions, it's also important to remain open-minded about progress, because the change that comes with new people and new ideas can make a positive difference.

BACK IN THE SADDLE AGAIN: Despite the box-office failure of the Duke's first Western feature, John Wayne took what work he could find in the era's inexpensively produced juvenile items.   *Courtesy: Warner Bros.*

SOMEWHERE IN SONORA (1933)

Director: Mack V. Wright
Screenwriters: Will Levington Comfort and Joseph Anthony Roach
"It's my only chance to show Bob Leadly how much I appreciate what he's done for me."

John Bishop (Wayne) is the top hand on Bob Leadly's Arizona ranch and a rider to be reckoned with in local rodeos. But his success in a stagecoach race sours when it appears he fixed the outcome by damaging his competitor's wheelbase. The law is too quick to toss Bishop in jail, but his boss (Henry B. Walthall) risks all he owns to get the young employee out and clear the lad's name by proving that professional gamblers did the deed. Only then does Bishop learn that some time before, Bob's innocent son Bart, (Paul Fix), was himself set up for a crime. Terrified young Bart heads south of the border, where for the sake of survival he becomes involved with a vicious Anglo gang that allows their atrocities to be blamed on Sonora's peaceful Mexican citizens. With a pair of would-be comic sidekicks, Bishop heads down that way, posing as a notorious escaped criminal in hopes that the gang will eventually ask him to join. They do, then he and the deeply repentant Bart are forced to head out on a violent raid against ranchers who resist this empire of evil.

THE MESSAGE: Anyone can say "thank you," perhaps even mean it. But when it comes to obligations, actions speak louder than words.

AN OATER WITH SOMETHING SPECIAL: Though technically just another B movie, this notably action-packed early Wayne vehicle fans has always held a special place in the hearts of fans of this form. *Courtesy: Warner Bros.*

THE MODERN D'ARTAGNAN: Duke enrolled as the fourth musketeer in this well-mounted Saturday morning serial about a flying ace who teams up with three veteran Foreign Legionnaires for contemporary African exploits. *Courtesy: Mascot*

THE THREE MUSKETEERS (1933)

Directors: Colbert Clark and Armand Schaefer
Screenwriter: Norman S. Hall
"All for one, and one for all!"

A big problem for small Hollywood companies was that their tight budgets did not permit them to bid against the majors for the most important new novels. The solution was to rely on tried-and-true stories. The work of Alexandre Dumas was made to order, since his books—including the 1844 classic that lends this film its title—were in the public domain. Screenwriter Hall and his team merely updated the old tale from Renaissance France to the contemporary desert. In Africa a modern incarnation of the three title characters—played by Jack Mulhall, Raymond Hatton, and Ralph Bushman—enter into a series of adventures that parallel those of Athos, Porthos, and Aramis. They even have their own D'Artagnan, named Tom Wayne (Duke), an American aviator who buzzes by overhead and then joins them in their exploits. Some things never change, though, and that includes the words of wisdom Dumas's own musketeers chanted, echoed here by the four heroes.

THE MESSAGE: Rugged individualism is fine to a degree, but don't ever underestimate loyalty to one's true friends, who will do or die for you.

HIS PRIVATE SECRETARY (1933)

Director: Philip H. Whitman
Screenwriters: Lewis D. Collins, Sam Katzman, and Jack Francis Natteford
"That's the kind of girl we need—a girl with a mind of her own."

It wasn't all B Westerns for Wayne during the early 1930s, as this minor league but charming romantic comedy proves. Duke is here effectively cast against type as Dick Wallace, a spoiled, lazy, rich brat who runs around with 1920s-type flapper-vamps. He suddenly changes attitudes and directions, leaving the big city to run a filling station in a small town after becoming infatuated with Marion Hall (Evalyn Knapp), an old-fashioned minister's daughter. They secretly marry, but Dick's dad (Reginald Barlow), who thinks the two are still dating, assumes his son has fallen prey to some gold digger. To prove herself (Marion married Dick unaware of his family's fortune), she goes to work as the secretary to old Mr. Wallace. However conventional and conservative Marion may be otherwise, she's forward thinking as far as business acumen goes and takes charge, to the delight of Mr. Wallace. Gazing at a picture of his late wife, Dick's dad sighs that this young lady reminds him of her and, as such, is precisely what he wanted for Junior. Finally the couple can reveal that they are married, and Dick comes to realize his seemingly stuffy father was right all along: He has found a solid but non-submissive woman.

THE MESSAGE: Flashiness may be fun for a fling, but when it comes time to marry, find a girl just like the girl who married dear old Dad!

MOVING BEYOND GENRE: To the surprise of many who perceived Wayne as typecast in action-adventure roles, in *His Private Secretary* he excelled as a young man of big business; the Duke displayed talent at both comedy and drama. *Courtesy: Colam Pictures*

THE MAN FROM MONTEREY (1933)

Director: Mack V. Wright
Screenwriter: Leslie Mason
"Herd him for the corral, and the rest will follow."

In yet another of Duke's B Westerns for Warner Bros./Four Star (as compared to the low-grade junk films in which he'd shortly appear), the star plays Capt. John Holmes, who is assigned to deal with a chaotic situation in California in the aftermath of the Mexican-American War. Many Spanish citizens feel isolated, angry, and threatened, certainly not without good reason. The drama derives from a U.S. government decision that all ranches must be newly registered, including those owned by aristocratic dons from long-ago land grants. Many refuse to comply, considering such a demand to be outrageous and insulting to their dignity. The problem is, if they don't do as ordered, their ranches may well be confiscated by opportunists and profiteers, both Anglo and Mexican. Holmes receives orders to head into that territory and make sure these noble people are not deprived of their rights. But first he asks his commander for the name of the most important, influential, and impertinent of the great rancheros. Before Holmes leaves the fort and heads off to face this man first (and shortly romance the fellow's lovely daughter), he directs this line at his commanding officer.

THE MESSAGE: Always tackle the largest and seemingly most difficult parts of a job first. However challenging, once that's completed, everything else will more easily fall into place.

SAGEBRUSH TRAIL (AKA *AN INNOCENT MAN*) (1933)

Director: Armand Schaefer
Screenwriter: Lindsley Parsons
"You'll be seeing me."

If Duke's films for Four Star/Warner Bros. were low-budget, the next round—for Poverty Row company Lone Star—would have to be considered grade Z in terms of production values. Still, Wayne gave them his all (a professional never phones in a performance), which is why they remain watchable today. In this film he's John Brant, who was sent to prison for a crime he did not commit. In addition to avoiding the lawman on his trail, Brant hopes to track down and kill the man who actually committed that now long-ago murder for which Brant served time. An easygoing outlaw (Lane Chandler) helps the Duke get away from pursuers, then convinces the head of his outlaw gang (Yakima Canutt, who also performed the movie's impressive horse stunts) to take in the newcomer. Soon the two pals are competing for the hand of a pretty town girl (Nancy Shubert), who enjoys all the attention so much that she even helps the two swains to stay clear of the law. Then it hits Brant like lightning: His new saddle pal is the guy he's sworn to shoot down. Though the old biblical line "Vengeance is mine, sayeth the Lord" never appears here, that's the underlying theme as Brant leaves such just deserts to higher powers.

THE MESSAGE: The ability to forgive is not a weakness, but a strength. On the other hand, never, ever forget.

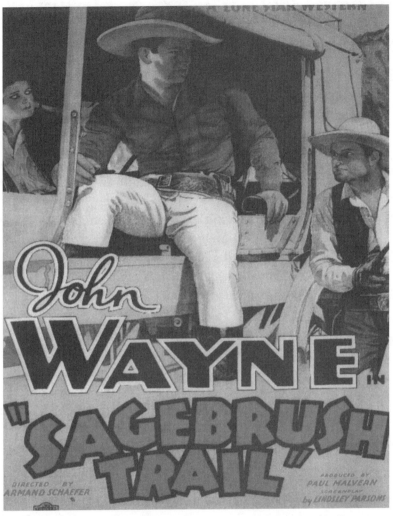

PULP FICTION, WESTERN STYLE: The advertising poster for this film
vividly reveals the great impact of dime novels (dating back to Ned
Buntline) and contemporary paperbacks on the Western film.
Courtesy: Lone Star

BLUE STEEL (1934)

Director and screenwriter: Robert N. Bradbury
"I'm glad you decided to drift along with me. It's kind of lonesome tracking alone."

Wayne is thought of as a rugged individualist, proving the theory that he who travels fastest travels alone. Well, maybe. Fact of the matter is, fastest isn't necessarily best. There's nothing like good company, in this case the definitive sidekick of B Westerns, George "Gabby" Hayes. Here Gabby plays an old-time sheriff who, like the Duke's character, John Carruthers, senses that dastardly deeds in an isolated town are being carried out by seemingly respectable people. Here's another of those oaters that reveal the black-hatted villain theory is but a myth. More often than not, bad guys are identified by fine-tailored suits. No matter how individualistic we may perceive the Western hero as being in general—and the John Wayne persona in particular—things work out a lot better when friends are around. In most of Wayne's early starring roles, those friends might be Gabby or stuntman Yakima Canutt doing double-duty as Duke's Indian pal Yak. In *The Three Mesquiteers* franchise, Wayne had two saddle pals. Even his embittered loner in *The Searchers*, who first berates young Jeff Hunter when the mixed-race youth wants to tag along on the quest to find a girl stolen by the Comanches, learns to like the fellow's company, eventually adopting him as a kind of unofficial foster son.

THE MESSAGE: Proudly keep your own vigil when that's necessary, but never turn away good company, which enriches your existence.

BEST OF THE Bs: Amid the plethora of low-budget films in which Wayne appeared, few stand out as memorably as *Blue Steel*, thanks to superior writing, well-staged action, and the ever stronger screen presence of the Duke. *Courtesy: Paul Malvern Prods./Monogram*

THE LUCKY TEXAN (1934)

Director and screenwriter: Robert N. Bradbury
"I'm going off to buy a Delmonico steak for a dog."

This better-than-average oater from Poverty Row studio Lone Star contains one truly memorable action sequence. Young Duke (more correctly, stunt double Yakima Canutt), chasing an outlaw by horseback, fails to make the legendary "leap" when attempting to pull the fleeing scoundrel off his horse. Our hero, Jerry Mason, rolls down a steep hill, his pursuit seemingly ended. No way! Jerry picks himself up, dusts himself off, and takes a shortcut by employing a nearby log to guide his ski-like plunge (without skis, of course, only cowboy boots) down a mining sluice cut into the mountain. Jerry heads the villain off at the pass, climbs a tree, and then jumps down from a branch (Canutt standing in once again) to knock the fleeing man off his mount, this time successfully. The bad guys here want the gold that Jerry and his old partner, Jack Benson (played by George "Gabby" Hayes), are profiting from after their dog, Friday, digs up a nugget and turns it over to the fellas. Half kidding, Jerry states that if they do get lucky and find more, he'll buy the mongrel a choice piece of meat. Well, the rich ore is there, so the sidekicks head into town to trade it in for cold cash. As soon as they do, the dog's master makes clear his words were not empty. Jerry's next stop: the butcher shop!

THE MESSAGE: Always keep your word, even when such sentiments were spoken in jest . . . and even if they were spoken to a dog.

WEST OF THE PECOS: Though not a Lone Star native, Wayne would gradually come to symbolize the rugged individualism and libertarian attitudes associated with what then qualified as our largest continental state.   *Courtesy: Paul Malvern Prods./Monogram*

THE STAR PACKER (1934)

Director and screenwriter: Robert N. Bradbury
"And don't be afraid to use it."

Not many people recall that before George Hayes became "Gabby," greatest of all B Western sidekicks, he played a variety of roles, including the villain in this Lone Star/Monogram featurette. Matlock is a seemingly friendly rancher who, as "the Shadow," secretly runs an empire of outlaws. When niece Anita (Verna Hillie) arrives on the scene, Matlock figures the best way to get rid of her, short of killing a family member, is to scare the girl away. He fills her head with ghost stories, claiming the area is haunted. But Duke's character, lawman John Travers, has a simple solution: Give the lovely lady her own gun. Her reply to Travers's warning: "I won't be!" Later, gang members dress up as animal-headed demons, thinking that'll frighten her. Instead she whips out her pistol and blasts away—sending the varmints scattering—and then, calm, cool, and collected, she heads back to bed. John is so proud of Anita that instead of riding off into the sunset, he marries her (offscreen). The final scene, five years after, has the two of them bringing up a child, though their little boy (dressed in full Indian regalia) prefers John's Native American pal Yak (Yakima Canutt) to his dad as a mentor.

THE MESSAGE: In movies, as in life, only the bad guys undervalue women or think they need to be looked after. The true male hero is enlightened enough to empower the women around him.

WHODUNIT? Despite its humble production values, this cleverly plotted B movie entertained audiences owing to a unique twist: It combined the oater stereotypes and settings with a mystery tale worthy of Agatha Christie. *Courtesy: Paul Malvern Prods./Monogram*

PARADISE CANYON (1935)

Director: Carl Pierson
Screenwriters: Robert Emmett Tansey and Lindsley Parsons
"I'm just a cowboy, driftin' from town to town."

From Monogram, another of those bargain-basement companies where Wayne found journeyman work during the Great Depression, came this most engaging adventure story. Duke plays a recently released convict tracking down his onetime partner, who framed our hero on counterfeiting charges. As John Wayne plays John Wyatt and the villain, Curly, is enacted by Yakima Canutt, there's an outside possibility that this mini-epic was influenced by the Earp/Brocious feud in real-life Tombstone. The plot has Wyatt joining Doc Carter's medicine show as a sharpshooter, appearing with that old-timer's daughter (Marion Burns) to lure customers for her dad's blend of bottled herbs and vitamins. Though she's certainly beautiful enough to attract any of the moneyed men in the towns the trio passes through, that hardly dissuades Wyatt from courting her. Like the star-in-embryo playing him, John Wyatt understands that it doesn't matter much what he does, just so long as he takes pride in his work, however humble it may be.

THE MESSAGE: It's important to take pride in your work and give it all you've got, no matter how everyday the task may be. Your dedication surely will pay off in the end.

THE LONE RIDER: In later years Wayne reflected that most of his lawmen were based on the real-life Wyatt Earp. Here he's named Wyatt, his best friend is Doc (derived from John Holliday), and their worst enemy is Curly (a nod to Bill Brocious). *Courtesy: Paul Malvern Prods./Monogram*

TEXAS TERROR (1935)

Director and screenwriter: Robert N. Bradbury
"Circumstantial evidence has convicted many a man."

In one of Lone Star's most tightly budgeted films, Duke plays John Higgins, the recently elected sheriff of a small cow town. Following a robbery, he pursues the outlaws and in the process accidentally kills a close friend, Old Dan (played by Frank Ball), or so he's led to believe. Worse, the deceased fella appears to have been part of the outlaw gang. John utters the above line even as he quits his job, allowing another pal (George "Gabby" Hayes) to wear the badge. In Wayne's first character role, Higgins becomes something of a hermit on horseback, complete with an obviously fake beard, roaming the frontier. Always, though, he clings to a deep belief that his pal was set up, even though he has no way to prove it—until the deceased man's sister returns to town. With her help, along with that of the new sheriff and Higgins's Indian friends (he's the only person in the area who appreciates their true worth), he finally clears himself of that killing (by proving that the bad guys framed him) while also setting the record straight on Old Dan. There's a little less action than usual here, and the budget was so tight that the extras who play farmers and ranch hands had to wear their own contemporary street clothes in the barn dance and cow-milking contest scene!

THE MESSAGE: As Rudyard Kipling aptly said, "If you can keep your head while all about you are losing theirs and blaming it on you . . . you'll be a Man, my son!" Things aren't always what they seem. And being a man is less about flexing muscles than searching for the truth.

RAINBOW VALLEY (1935)

Director: Robert N. Bradbury
Screenwriter: Lindsley Parsons
"I took engineering in school."

The citizens of a small, isolated town (presumably based on Rainbow Valley, Arizona) are attempting to build a road that will link them to the outside world. Standing against this modernization is an outlaw gang that knows such progress will end their reign of terror. When John Martin (Duke) arrives on the scene (he's presumably a drifter but actually a government man), those in charge are impressed by his courage in fighting the lawless elements and his willingness to whip the locals into an army of citizen-soldiers. These include George (played by George "Gabby" Hayes), who drives a dilapidated car called Nellie, a precursor of Pat Brady's warmly remembered Jeep Nellybelle on TV's *Roy Rogers Show* during the 1950s. The film serves as a forerunner of later big-budget projects such as *McLintock!* and *Chisum*, in which John Wayne's character, contrary to his popular image, reveals himself to be a progressive by standing up against reactionary forces. Still, John Martin's courage is not enough to get the job done; someone with scientific knowledge is necessary to complete a road—which is when, surprisingly, this seeming vagabond reveals that he's in fact perfectly qualified to oversee this task.

THE MESSAGE: Never undervalue the worth of a college education, and never think that the skills taught at institutions of higher learning conflict with the image of a "man's man."

THE DESERT TRAIL (1935)

Director: Lewis D. Collins
Screenwriter: Lindsley Parsons
"It's talk that gets you into trouble with a woman—they're always thinkin' you mean more than you say."

Here's one for the guys! The main plot of this rodeo circuit comedy-drama involves John Scott and his friendly-enemy saddle pal Kansas Charlie (Eddy Chandler) trying to escape a posse that mistakenly believes the boys have robbed a pay station and killed a man in the process. The grifters spend a lot more time, though, attempting to deal with several gorgeous women they meet along the way. (For what it's worth, the trail runs through a prairie, and there are no deserts in sight.) First up is Juanita (Carmen Laroux), a lovely Latina who plays one guy off the other (several other men enter the mix as well) and considers only their bankrolls while trying to choose between them. Our antiheroes head off in a different direction, soon running into pretty, perky Anne (Mary Kornman), who actually takes such things as character into consideration. Even here, however, it's difficult to know what to say around a woman, as the beguiled men come to realize that each lovely lady is going to filter the men's words through her own unique female sensibility. At one point in the movie, Duke's sidekick actually tries to keep his mouth entirely shut whenever a woman comes into view!

THE MESSAGE: You may have heard the expression "The man who understands women." Well, if he exists—if!—assume it isn't you. Watch what you say, because it WILL be held against you.

HARD RIDER: Fans of Wayne's early mini-epics mostly agree the Duke provided his most impressive horseback sequences in *The Desert Trail* and, seen here, *The New Frontier. Courtesy: mptvimages.com*

THE DAWN RIDER (1935)

Director: Robert N. Bradbury
Screenwriter: Lloyd Nosler
"You and whose army?"

This may be the best B Western young Wayne ever made, thanks to
a smart story that had been filmed before (*Gallopin' Through* in 1923)
and would be twice again (*Western Trails* in 1941 and *Dawn Rider* in
2012). This time around Duke is John Mason, who heads to his home-
town after getting into a fight with a fella named Ben (Reed Howes).
As it ends in a draw, they become friends, and when John is wounded
by robbers at his dad's place (and his father is killed), Ben offers to
help John mend. Problem is, Ben's girl Alice Gordon (Marion Burns),
while nursing John, falls in love with him. John hopes to recover and
go after the villain who killed his dad. His next big problem: The villain, Rudd Gordon (Dennis Moore), is Alice's brother! When the final
showdown comes around, a jealous Ben secretly removes the bullets
from John's gun as our hero heads out at high noon to face off with
Rudd. Sound intriguing? Wouldn't spoil the fun for you by giving
away a twist ending worthy of Hitchcock.

*THE MESSAGE: Always imitate Duke's reply to Ben when that false
friend threatens to knock him over. Even if you're hurting, don't let the
other guy know it, and you'll beat him yet.*

BORN TO THE WEST (AKA HELL TOWN) (1937)

Director: Charles Barton
Screenwriters: Robert Yost and Stuart Anthony (screenplay based on the novel *Hell Town* by Zane Grey)
"I don't like branding—it hurts in the wrong place."

Another low-budget oater, this Paramount B movie (as compared to the C-minus items Duke had been appearing in for Lone Star) marked a step up in status, thanks to a solid studio director, a script derived from a Zane Grey novel, and lavish stock footage from an earlier silent version of the story. Wayne is Dave Rudd, the black sheep of a Montana ranch family, who accepts a job from his older cousin (John Mack Brown) while hoping to win a lovely lady (Marsha Hunt). To accomplish this he must successfully drive their cattle to the railhead (despite a menacing outlaw gang) and bring the money back rather than lose it all in a gambling den. Dave is addicted to poker and believes himself to be a top player, bragging that he's the best "west of the Mississippi." Yet toward the end of this coming-of-age tale, Dave finally admits his boast was empty. He's been living out a fantasy of freedom. Redemption is his at the end once he grasps that, however true the above epithet may be for a footloose young man, it would be tragic to carry that attitude past a certain point in life. After all, in the film's final shot, Dave Rudd is more than happy to get branded with his first serious full-time job and the enduring love of a great woman.

THE MESSAGE: Although many will excuse you for sowing your wild oats while you're young, it's to your advantage to recall some sage advice: When you become a man, you must put aside childish things.

THREE TEXAS STEERS (1939)

Director: George Sherman
Screenwriters: Betty Burbridge and Stanley Roberts
"I'm a cowhand, ma'am. I chase cows."

In one of the final *Three Mesquiteers* mini-oaters from Mascot Pictures, produced just before John Ford made a superstar out of Wayne with *Stagecoach*, he once again plays Stony Brooke, the good-natured Westerner who rides with grim Ray "Crash" Corrigan as Tucson Smith and comedic Max Terhune as Lullaby Joslin. They meet a gorgeous circus owner (Carole Landis, who a year later would play the blond cavewoman opposite Victor Mature in *1,000,000 B.C.*) in need of help. Seems her crooked partner wrecked the show, as he and his fellow buzzards have designs on the ranch young Nancy has inherited. Naturally, the boys want to strike a blow for what's right, and it sure doesn't hurt any that she's mighty pretty. The thing is, Duke knew even back then that it was better to be humble and honest than to put on airs. Eventually, the blonde takes a long look at him and sighs: "If I could only learn to moo!"

THE MESSAGE: It's who you are inside, now and forever, that counts, and not the job that you may be stuck with at the moment.

END OF THE B MOVIE TRAIL: As Stoney Brooke, Wayne rode with saddle-pals Max Terhune and Ray "Crash" Corrigan; shortly thereafter, Wayne would be catapulted to the big leagues thanks to *Stagecoach.*
Courtesy: Republic

STAGECOACH (1939)

Director: John Ford
Screenwriters: Ernest Haycox and Dudley Nichols
"You got no folks . . . neither have I. Well, I still got a ranch across the border . . . a man could live there . . . and a woman. Will you go?"

This grand tale of an odd assortment of characters crossing the desert with Geronimo in hot pursuit may have been loosely adapted from a French short story by Guy de Maupassant. But Ford, Wayne, and company transformed it into a definitive tale of the Arizona frontier. Wayne plays the Ringo Kid, who has escaped from prison to kill the no-goods that shot his brother. Along the way he meets Dallas (Claire Trevor), a soiled dove. As Dallas cares for the newborn baby of a cavalry officer's wife, Ringo notes the tender heart beneath her tough exterior. While respectable types regard Dallas as considerably lower than Ringo, he has no such moral compunctions but realizes that women stranded on the frontier often could find no other employment. Instead of standing in judgment of Dallas, Ringo admires her for her positive attributes. He also gets down to basics, fast. As demonstrated by Dallas' acceptance of this decidedly unromantic proposal, these two know better than to expect the nirvana that most young couples hope to achieve. When they ride off on a buggy toward Mexico, there seems to be no room for doubt that they will make a go of it.

THE MESSAGE: Accept people for who they are rather than judging them according to assumptions or prejudices—and that includes a potential spouse. Ask not whether that person is good enough for you, but whether you're both willing to do what it takes to make a marriage work.

TOWARD A MORE REALISTIC WESTERN: John Ford, always a stickler for detailed realism of costume, had no interest in a typical cowboy-gunfighter costume, insisting that Wayne as the Ringo Kid dress like a frontier farm-boy. *Courtesy: © Ned Scott / mptvimages.com*

ALLEGHENY UPRISING (1939)

Director: William A. Seiter
Screenwriter: P. J. Wolfson (screenplay based on a story by Neil H. Swanson)

"Men, we've fought and won. But in winning we have lost something. In defending one law, we've come to despise all law. And if we go on like this, we'll destroy the very thing we've been fighting for."

Allegheny Uprising features Wayne as the real-life patriot James Smith, who fought alongside the British during the French and Indian War. Upon returning to Pennsylvania, he and other settlers are discouraged to learn that a sleazy entrepreneur (Brian Donlevy) is trading guns and liquor to the Indians. The pioneers push for a law to prevent this, but a British officer (George Sanders) defends the now illegal trade. In retaliation, they begin the Black Boys Rebellion of 1765, a mini-prelude to the Revolutionary War. When the wagon train of supplies to hostile tribes is detained, the Professor (John F. Hamilton) articulates what James inwardly feels: There is a thin separation between freedom and chaos. When the Professor speaks this line, he's realized while it's imperative to stand up against tyranny and injustice, individual initiative must maintain a prominent place in the American landscape. At the same time, however, individual initiative must be balanced by community loyalty.

THE MESSAGE: Democracy is never an easy form of government to maintain, and common sense must prevail if the experiment that we refer to as a republic is to succeed. A delicate balance must be found between utter chaos and total conformity.

THE LONG VOYAGE HOME (1940)

Director: John Ford
Screenwriter: Dudley Nichols
"The best thing to do about memories is forget 'em."

What John Ford was to the Hollywood cinema—our greatest dramatic poet—Eugene O'Neill had been to the Broadway stage. Their precipitous meeting occurred with this Ford adaptation of four of O'Neill's one-act plays on the subject of the merchant marine: the singular breed that made up this unique profession, a legion of lost men as fabled as the French Foreign Legion, if less romanticized by pulp fiction and adventure filmmakers. Nichols updated the material to the very edge of the inevitable upcoming war, as a young Swede, Olsen (Wayne), learns the fatalistic view of life that underscores all activities by the other crewmen. "Red Sails in the Sunset," which would become one of the great musical ballads, mournfully plays in the background as the crew of the *Glencairn* fight among themselves until they come into contact with the forces of evil that even then were amassing to challenge democracy and the free world.

THE MESSAGE: Don't spend your time mulling on past mistakes. That only leads to madness. Instead, make things better in the present so that you can make a positive impact for the future.

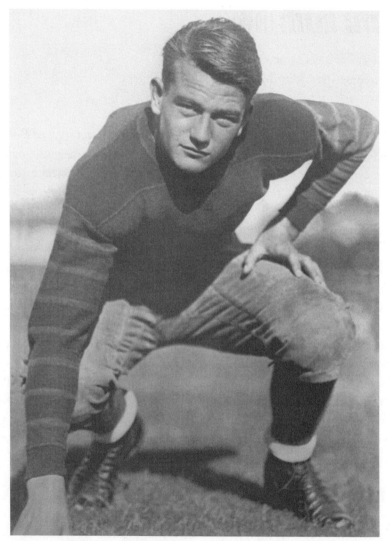

DIRECTED BY JOHN FORD: "Pappy" noticed John Wayne on the football field and sensed the youth had the charisma to be a true movie star. *Courtesy: mptvimages.com*

SEVEN SINNERS (1940)

Director: Tay Garnett
Screenwriters: John Meehan and Harry Tugend
"Yes, sir!"

Duke is Dan, a navy captain serving in the U.S. protectorate of Boni Komba in the South Seas. Like fellow "officer-and-a-gentleman" types, Dan leads a double life: attending officers' balls where they dance with classy, respectable ladies before sneaking off to low-life establishments to dally with women of the night. Dan makes the mistake of falling in love with Bijou (Marlene Dietrich) and plans to marry her. When his commanding officer (Reginald Denny) insists that such a move would destroy Dan's promising career, the young man insists: "It's my own personal, private business." Flattered by the implied proposal, Bijou—a whore with a heart of gold—knows that in time Dan's moon madness would give way to a realization that he's lost what he most wanted in life. She cares enough about Dan to slip away on the next boat out. Dan returns to active duty, at film's end saying those two simple words when his commander makes clear that it's time to clear his head of any romantic notions and get back to reality. At that moment Dan transforms from an overgrown boy to a young man, setting an impossible romance aside while rediscovering himself.

THE MESSAGE: The arrogance of youth is universal; All of us, women and men, suffer from it. The wisest among us come to realize that our elders, owing to their experience in the world, do know what's best for us in the long run. Respect them and their wisdom.

THREE FACES WEST (1940)

Director: Bernard Vorhaus
Screenwriters: F. Hugh Herbert, Joseph M. March, and Samuel Ornitz
"It's a free country."

The title aside, this is not a generic Western. John Phillips (Wayne) lives in a small, devastated Kansas farming community. Poverty, combined with wild winds and other natural disasters, has left the people sick in body as well as mind. Phillips convinces two European refugees, a doctor (Charles Coburn) and his pretty daughter (Sigrid Gurie), to leave New York, where they had relocated to escape fascism in their native Austria, and take the train out to the wide-open spaces. Though the dedicated Doc wants to stay on in the small town and help, the girl is intimidated by the shambles of a house she must cohabit with Phillips. In a disappointed drawl, he speaks the above line. Later, when he takes the government up on an offer to relocate the entire community to an area of Oregon where veteran farmers are scarce, John—though their leader—makes certain that everyone knows he or she can come along to hopefully happier pastures or stay behind. And when the pressure gets to him and he considers abandoning the entire project, the girl (by now a convert to his "way") tells him the same thing. He, being one more incarnation of the John Wayne persona, regains his momentum and heads on back to do his job.

THE MESSAGE: Americans cannot, in the world according to John Wayne, expect many entitlements, but there are a few. One is the right to vote; another, the freedom to always choose for yourself.

THE HERO: Wayne, who first had the opportunity to play a trailblazer in *The Big Trail* (seen here), once again leads pioneers cross-country, this time during the Great Depression in *Three Faces West*.
Courtesy: mptvimages.com

THE DARK COMMAND (1940)

Director: Raoul Walsh
Screenwriters: F. Hugh Herbert and Grover Jones
"I took an oath."

This film is special in many regards: Wayne is reunited with Walsh, who a decade earlier gave the Duke his first shot at A-list stardom; and two kings of the silver screen cowboys, Wayne and Roy Rogers, co-star, with George "Gabby" Hayes (often a sidekick to one or the other) following them both around while sputtering "authentic frontier gibberish." As to the title, dark is right! This tale of William Clark Quantrill (spelled "Cantrell" here, and played to perfection by Walter Pidgeon) in Bleeding Kansas of 1859–61 (a period marked by violence between free state and slave state settlers) forsakes Republic Pictures' big, beautiful look for its more ambitious oaters of the late 1930s, qualifying this as the first film noir Western, a subgenre that would flourish in the postwar years. Wayne's character, Bob Seton, is an easygoing grifter who settles in Lawrence and, to win the hand of a fair lady (Claire Trevor), runs for the office of marshal. When her kid brother (Roy) gets involved in a shooting, she and her father (Porter Hall) make clear they'll be forever grateful if only Seton will let the lad out of jail on bail. This, of course, is his big chance to marry the dream girl. Aware, though, that they have a horse ready to spirit her sibling across the border, Bob softly speaks the above words.

THE MESSAGE: Winning what you most want is important, but not if it's at the cost of your self-respect.

A MAN BETRAYED (1941)

Director: John H. Auer
Screenwriters: Jack Moffitt, Tom Kilpatrick, and Isabel Dawn
"If you borrow a cup of sugar, you should return a cup and a half."

This overlooked gem provided Duke with a delightful change of pace as Lynn Hollister, a small-town lawyer in rural Illinois whose best pal Johnny dies (either by suicide or murder) right after visiting a naughty nightclub in Chicago. Shortly, our fish-out-of-water hero arrives in the big city, anxious and eager to learn the truth. The problem is, after following a lead in the possible killing that runs all the way up the local ladder to a powerful crime boss (Edward Ellis), Lynn falls in love with that fat cat's gorgeous daughter (Frances Dee). This movie employs a combination of comedy and drama to comment on corruption behind the scenes of America's seemingly honest political institutions. Thanks to screenwriter Dawn, *A Man Betrayed* is so filled with fabulous one-liners that it's hard to choose only a few standouts. "Everybody has to start by knocking on some door . . . but they don't have to break them down," a character comments about Lynn's uncompromising attitudes. Duke proves otherwise. Another personal favorite: "It takes fourteen muscles to grin and fifty to frown. I guess I'm just plain lazy." Still, his line about borrowing sums up this main character's attitude.

THE MESSAGE: When someone comes through for you, you should always pay back more than you got. Doing so, without being asked to, is what constitutes that thing we call "character."

BREAKING THE MOLD: Wayne had appeared in so many Westerns, he couldn't help but wonder if he'd ever play a contemporary man again; he won such a role in the better-than-average melodrama, *A Man Betrayed*. *Courtesy: mptvimages.com*

THE SHEPHERD OF THE HILLS (1941)

Director: Henry Hathaway
Screenwriters: Grover Jones and Stuart Anthony (screenplay based
on a novel by Harold Bell Wright)
"The bigger the man, the deeper the imprint."

It isn't only physical size to which Wayne's character, Young Matt,
refers in the best Hollywood film ever made about America's hillbilly
subculture. That's due in large part to Harold Bell Wright, the novelist
who captured the essence of the Ozarks—the xenophobic people with
their unique values—without falling prey to romanticism or conde-
scension. Hathaway's breathtaking imagery enhances the film's reputation as a definitive screen study of a rigid society of scattered loners
attempting to deal with the arrival of an outsider (Harry Carey Sr.).
This soft-spoken stranger convinces most residents that he is heaven-
sent, a good shepherd tending to their spiritual and physical needs. Not
so with Young Matt, a dark, deeply troubled youth who lives in daily
anguish owing to a pressing memory: Sarah, his mother, was deserted
by the man who impregnated her and left her to die in childbirth, causing other mountaineers to view Matt not as one of their own but as
a Cain-like outcast. Matt has sworn to someday track down and kill
whoever it was that delivered such a melancholic figure into this hostile
world. Thanks to the stranger's mollifying effect and the adoration of a
girl (Betty Field), Matt sets bitterness aside and learns to forgive.

*THE MESSAGE: Being born big has its advantages, but with them
come special responsibilities. Once you realize the importance of the asser-
tion "Vengeance is mine, sayeth the Lord," you're on your way to becoming
big in spirit as well as size.*

IN OLD CALIFORNIA (1942)

Director: William C. McGann
Screenwriters: Gertrude Purcell, Frances Hyland, Gladys Atwater, and J. Robert Bren
"I like milk."

Tom Craig (Wayne) steps into a saloon and orders cow juice instead of rotgut. Local varmints are about to give this Boston-born greenhorn wearing a fancy suit a hard time—until he whips out a silver dollar and bends it in his bare hand. The tough guys back off, perhaps a wee bit wiser: Being a real man has nothing to do with one's drink of choice, nor is a university graduate any less manly than some self-confessed redneck. Shortly, Tom has two beautiful females competing for his hand: saloon dolly Lacey (Binnie Barnes) and the classy, high-born Ellen (Helen Parrish). Through his relationships with these women, Tom not only educates the citizenry as to the silliness of strict gender roles for guys, but also learns a lesson himself about women. Initially he rules out marriage with Lacey owing to her low social status. When an epidemic threatens to wipe out gold miners who in the past refused newcomer Tom's friendship, Ellen asks why he would now risk everything to bring them medicine. "They're people," he says. "They need help." When he arrives on the scene, Tom finds Lacey already there, nursing the sick. After the two save the day together, Tom wants her and her alone as a wife.

THE MESSAGE: Aristocracy in the new paradigm of America has nothing to do with social status at birth, but it has everything to do with the presence or absence of character.

A TURNING POINT: Before *The Spoilers*, most of Wayne's action heroes had been relatively simple men; finally, he proved he could play a far more complex character who is the clear predecessor of Ethan Edwards in *The Searchers* (seen here). *Courtesy: Warner Bros. / mptvimages.com*

THE SPOILERS (1942)

Director: Ray Enright
Screenwriters: Lawrence Hazard and Tom Reed (screenplay based on a novel of the same name by Rex Beach)
"You'd look good to me, baby, in a burlap bag."

The link between John Wayne and Gary Cooper as the true kings of adult-oriented Westerns is cemented by this stylish adaptation of Rex Beach's 1905 novel about the Alaska gold rush. In the 1930 version (the third of five), Cooper—who had been Raoul Walsh's original choice for *The Big Trail* and also was considered by John Ford for *Stagecoach*—played Roy Glennister, here essayed by the Duke. Tragically, the desire of these two giants to work together in Sam Peckinpah's *Ride the High Country* (1962) came to a quick end when Cooper passed away. In both versions of *The Spoilers*, each actor was well cast as one more of those rugged men each played with such seeming effortlessness. And like many other Wayne projects both before and after this one, the theme was populist in orientation, with the bad guys once again raw capitalists who rose to the top of society by immoral shenanigans. When not defending his mine from such would-be claim jumpers, and before the classic final fight sequence with the worst man in a suit (Randolph Scott), Roy has a chance to reignite still-flickering flames of desire with a former lover, Cherry Malotte (Marlene Dietrich). He speaks the above quote when she dresses to the hilt in order to excite him, only to realize he's already there.

THE MESSAGE: Trimmings are fine and dandy, but at Thanksgiving what we most look forward to is the bird itself.

PITTSBURGH (1942)

Director: Lewis Seiler
Screenwriters: Kenneth Gamet, Tom Reed, George Owen, and John Twist

"There isn't a thing in the world I can't do if I set my mind to it."

Six months after *The Spoilers*, Wayne, Randolph Scott, and Marlene Dietrich were reunited for this virtual replay set in 1930s Pennsylvania, with coal and steel here substituting for gold. The male stars reverse their roles, with Duke the heavy here, allowing Randy to win their inevitable fistfight. Charles "Pittsburgh" Markham, an ambitious poor boy, makes this claim to pal Cash Evans (Scott) and to Josie (Dietrich), the girl they both love. Boast degenerates into hubris once Markham forgoes his earlier humility. In pursuit of the American dream, he becomes corrupted, forgetting the social contract he made with fellow workers who, unlike him, did not possess the genius to rise up and out of the tunnels and shafts. The promises Markham had made to his employees, such as building pleasant communal living quarters, are conveniently forgotten or endlessly put off. The film does not celebrate such raw capitalism (the practice of capitalism without a conscience), but criticizes it as Markham ultimately learns that friendship—to a guy or a girl—matters more than anything. Fortunately, Markham is rescued from his self-made morass when, as World War II begins, he discovers altruism, setting aside his rugged individualism to instead pursue honor in self-sacrifice.

THE MESSAGE: Striving for success is fine, but take heed of what Jackie Gleason once said: "Be nice to all those little people you meet on the way up, because you're gonna meet 'em all again on the way back down!"

FLYING TIGERS (1942)

Director: David Miller
Screenwriters: Kenneth Gamet and Barry Travers
"Results around here are based on cooperation and understanding."

As mentioned earlier, Duke is warmly recalled by many of his fans as the ultimate screen incarnation of rugged individualism, American-style. Despite how often he portrayed that character type, always his heroes have grasped the need for community values as well, particularly during terrible times in which events beyond our control threaten the very future of our nation—and that very rugged individualism so essential to American ideology. Then the old "We must all hang together or we will all hang separately" adage comes into play. Here Wayne is Capt. Jim Gordon, one of Gen. Claire Chennault's volunteers fighting the Japanese in China before America officially entered the war. "I can't have grandstanders trying to hog the whole show," he tells Woody (John Carroll) after the ace pilot takes off on his own. "I thought it was every man for himself," Woody answers in honest surprise. No way! "Discipline in the air is strict," Captain Gordon continues, "because it's the only way an outfit like this can operate." In time Woody acquiesces and redeems his earlier hotshot attitudes by making the full and final sacrifice. Wayne then welcomes new volunteers into the group who'll take up the slack.

THE MESSAGE: The stars on our flag symbolize the independence of individual statehood, while the stripes represent the original thirteen colonies that banded together to create a unified country. Only through a balance between the two extremes will our way of life survive and succeed.

REAP THE WILD WIND (1942)

Director: Cecil B. DeMille
Screenwriters: Charles Bennett, Alan Le May, and Jeanie Macpherson
"I'm not interested in excuses—I'm interested in performance."

This seafaring tale, set mostly in the Florida Keys circa 1840, features Duke in what appears to be a tailor-made part (a rugged sea captain)—only to turn him from a role model hero into a tragic figure. Wayne's character, Capt. Jack Stuart, hopes to show the commodore (Walter Hampden) that he can in time take over their seafaring company. His only competition is lawyer Stephen Tolliver (Ray Milland), who has been rejected by Loxi (Paulette Goddard), the feisty woman they both love. "I'm going to marry a *real* man," Loxi tells Steve, referring to Captain Jack. Only things don't turn out that way. When Jack loses ship and valuable cargo on a dangerous reef, he tries to explain why it isn't his fault and then fails to listen to his boss when that wise old man speaks the above words. Given a second chance, Jack squanders it, throwing in his lot with a criminal (Raymond Massey) who sabotages ships and then salvages the valuables aboard. Duke redeems himself by fighting a giant squid (and dying) to save Steve's life. In the final shot that fine-dressed fellow heads off on a honeymoon with the girl who ultimately realized that men, like books, ought not to be judged by their covers.

THE MESSAGE: Being a "real man" has less to do with how tall you stand than how big a person you are inside. Most important, never whine: Do your work well, and you will win.

DOWN TO THE SEA IN SHIPS: One reason Wayne was so effective at playing seafaring men is that he was a seasoned sailor himself; here, he relaxes on his yacht *The Wild Goose* with son Ethan in 1966.   *Courtesy: mptvimages.com*

A LADY TAKES A CHANCE (1943)

Director: William A. Seiter
Screenwriters: Robert Ardrey, Jo Swerling, and Garson Kanin
"Anything that ties you down is no good."

Here's a classic Wayne quote that must be set in context if it is to be understood. Duke plays rodeo cowboy Duke Hudkins. It hardly seems likely that the Duke-as-Duke thing is coincidental: Having achieved A-movie superstardom, Wayne could now go about forging his unique iconic image as one of the big screen's leading man's man action heroes. Here, though, aside from a few barroom brawls, there's little violence and lots of sophisticated comedy of the screwball order. As Molly J. Truesdale, Jean Arthur shines as a sweetly sexy New Yorker who heads west on a bus tour in large part because the men she meets back east just don't make the grade. Arthur and Wayne "meet cute" when a bucking bronco tosses him into her lap. But roping this cowboy won't be so easy. "Women are like socks," his philosophy goes, so "you got to change 'em regular." His grizzly sidekick Waco (Charles Winninger) warns the girl: "Love is the best thing there is, but you're barking up the wrong cowboy." Apparently Duke can only be loyal to his rugged mount, Sammy. The point is, once Molly has returned home, Duke—finally realizing what he's lost—changes his tune mighty fast, pursues her, and brings her back to live with him in the wide-open spaces.

THE MESSAGE: Free and footloose is a great way to live, while you're still a kid. Stick with that too long, though, and you'll end up a lonely old man.

WAR OF THE WILDCATS (AKA *IN OLD OKLAHOMA*) (1943)

Director: Albert S. Rogell
Screenwriters: Thomson Burtis, Ethel Hill, and Eleanore Griffin
"I've been raised around Indians, seen them pushed and squeezed out of what was theirs. If my helping them gets half of what belongs to them is 'fantastic,' then that's what I am."

President Theodore Roosevelt (Sidney Blackmer) must sit in judgment as to which of two would-be entrepreneurs will receive the oil rights on land that includes a Native American reservation. A slick man in a suit, Jim Gardner (Albert Dekker), has offered to give the Indians 12.5 percent of the profits. One of T.R.'s "Rough Riders," cowboy Dan Somers (Duke), proposes that 50 percent of everything ought to go to the tribal council. Somers represents a group of out-of-work dirt farmers, small-timers banding together, each tossing what little he has into the pot, a workers' collective. When Gardner all but accuses them of being communists, Somers makes clear that that's not the case. As their leader he will receive 1 percent for his contributions. If the plan works, that'll be a lot of money. He deserves as well as wants it. But unlike his adversary Gardner, Dan is not thinking only about profits. As Duke's character would later say in *The Alamo*, "There's right and there's wrong." According to Somers, making sure everyone makes a decent profit, even if the guy at the top will do slightly better than the rest of them, is right. So is guaranteeing that our first Americans finally get a fair shake at the American dream.

THE MESSAGES: (1) Capitalism is fine, though only when it is practiced within certain moral confines. (2) Despite their rocky past, cowboys and Indians can work together.

NOW, AN "A" WESTERN STAR: During the 1940s, Wayne remained loyal to the Western genre, only now the films were of a far higher quality. *Courtesy: mptvimages.com*

THE FIGHTING SEABEES (1944)

Director: Edward Ludwig
Screenwriters: Borden Chase and Aeneas MacKenzie
"We build so that others can fight? Uh-uh! We fight for what we build!"

Here is yet another of those highly propagandistic pro-war films that all the studios in Hollywood began churning out immediately after Pearl Harbor, in which each aspect of the armed forces, as well as civilian contributions at home, were lauded as doing their fair share for the greater cause. Members of the naval construction battalions, better known as the Seabees, were unique and worthy of their own tribute, offered here, as these were civilians who had to build constructions in the South Pacific to house the military men once they claimed an island, as well as bulldoze jungle areas to create runways for planes to land and take off again at a moment's notice. It's important to note that much of the story line here is (to be kind) "fanciful," though at the time audiences took what they saw as a combination of documentary and gospel. The Duke plays Lt. Cmdr. Wedge Donovan, who competes with a military man (Dennis O'Keefe) for the hand of a feisty lady volunteer (the fascinating Susan Hayward). He also wants to know why his men are not allowed to wear weapons and use them if the enemy should attack. The above quote makes clear his views on the subject.

THE MESSAGE: Certain regulations are useless if they don't allow men (and women!) who volunteer to work in the line of fire to be able to defend themselves.

TALL IN THE SADDLE (1944)

Director: Edwin L. Marin
Screenwriters: Michael Hogan, Paul Fix, and Gordon Ray Young
"I never feel sorry for what happens to a woman."

Claims that John Wayne was misogynistic, an attitude expressed through characters like Rocklin in this noirish Western, are seemingly evidenced by the above quote. To be fair, these words must be considered in context. This film may well have inspired Akira Kurosawa to make *Yojimbo* (1961), the samurai thriller that served as progenitor for *A Fistful of Dollars* (1964), Sergio Leone's initial spaghetti Western, the movie that established Clint Eastwood as the greatest Western star since the Duke. Here antihero/loner Rocklin stumbles into a particularly nasty little town where two factions are fighting for total control. Both gangs are run by women, the recently arrived Arleta (Ella Raines) and the equally pretty, equally indomitable and strong-willed Clara (Audrey Long). Even as the opposing sides attempt to manipulate Rocklin for their own ends, he turns the tables on each.

THE MESSAGE: With equal rights go equal responsibilities. Any woman who steps onto a traditionally male playing field shouldn't expect men to take pity on her if things don't work out according to her plans.

THEY WERE EXPENDABLE (1945)

Director: John Ford (Captain, U.S.N.R.)
Screenwriter: Frank "Spig" Wead (screenplay based on a novel of the same name by William L. White)
"Theirs is not to reason why, theirs but to do . . ."

This is the finest World War II movie made while combat still flared. Though released as the war came to an end, the idea had been to create one more propaganda piece for the cause, in this case about the PT (patrol torpedo) boat squadrons ("high-powered canoes," as they were unkindly called by many marines) that, mosquito-like, annoyed the Japanese as a delaying tactic during 1942, until General MacArthur could indeed return. As compared to most films of that period, Ford's is without bombast or overstatement: a quiet, sincere, noble work based on William L. White's documentation of courage and sacrifice. Initially Wayne's Lt. (j.g.) Rusty Ryan expresses disappointment at running messages rather than being in the thick of the fighting. Until, that is, another lieutenant (Robert Montgomery) reminds him of those old lines from Tennyson about the job of any soldier (or sailor, or marine) in any war: ". . . and die," Rusty says, completing the quote.

THE MESSAGE: In life, as in war, the big picture is complex. Only a few people get to shine. To quote another poet, Browning, "they also serve" who do the grunt work, without which victory could not be achieved.

WORKING WITH THE MASTER: Arguably the greatest of all World War II films, the masterpiece *They Were Expendable* reunited Wayne with his mentor, John Ford; the two are pictured here in 1966.
Courtesy: mptvimages.com

DAKOTA (1945)

Director: Joseph Kane
Screenwriters: Lawrence Hazard, Howard Estabrook, and Carl Foreman
"I learned one thing from General Mouton: When you're surrounded and there isn't a chance? Attack!"

Several years following the Civil War, former Confederate John Devlin (Duke) elopes with the young daughter, Sandy (Vera Ralston), of a Chicago railroad magnate. He wants to head for California, but she insists on pushing north to Fargo. Sandy has privileged information that the railroad will be heading up there next; also, she lifted twenty thousand dollars from her pop's safe so they can buy up the land that surveyors have marked out for the tracks to cross. Who was it that claimed that every great fortune begins with a crime? What makes these newlyweds the good guys and a competing outfit led by Jim Bender (Ward Bond) the baddies is that the Devlins want to generously pay wheat farmers for their land while their opponents plan to burn the sodbusters out and blame the raids on nearby peaceful Indians. We root for the lesser of two evils, if only via situation ethics. The point is that the Devlins' (relatively) honest plans put them at the mercy of the Bender gang. Shortly, all hope of survival (much less success) appears lost. That's when John decides that the only way to win is by recalling his career as a soldier, taking sage advice from his commander and now treating everyday life as he once did the field of combat.

THE MESSAGE: Being a victim is not a life situation but a state of mind. No matter how bad the odds might appear, if you believe you can win, then you can. Attitude is everything!

A WANDERER OF THE WASTELANDS: Some of Wayne's best roles have cast him as a loner drawn into the problems of decent folk in need of a hero; that's true of Duke's parts in *Dakota* and, seen here, *Hondo*. Courtesy: Warner Bros. / © Bud Fraker / mptvimages.com

BACK TO BATAAN (1945)

Director: Edward Dmytryk
Screenwriters: Ben Barzman and Richard H. Landau
"I shall return."

In real life Gen. Douglas MacArthur made that statement as he left Corregidor following the fall of Bataan. In this film Wayne's character serves as something of a stand-in for that commander. He and an invisible army (that was always the film's working title) made up of Philippine volunteers (their leader played by Anthony Quinn) and a ragtag group of American survivors hold out for as long as possible. Then they embody the famous Shakespearean quote that Wayne would speak in *The Alamo:* "Sometimes discretion is the better part of valor." The wise man knows how effective it can be to allow the enemy to win a Pyrrhic and temporary victory so that they will in time lose the war. Intended as one more propaganda piece for the cause, the film wasn't released until after the war ended. That explains why images of actual U.S. Army Rangers being freed from the Japanese prison camp on Cabanatuan were included as a prologue for postwar audiences.

THE MESSAGE: As Gen. Francis Marion said way back during the Revolutionary War, "He who fights and runs away lives to fight another day."

TYCOON (1947)

Director: Richard Wallace
Screenwriters: Borden Chase and John Twist (screenplay based on a novel of the same name by C. E. Scoggins)
"It isn't a matter of 'contract.' It's about common decency."

One year before *Red River,* Wayne starred in this contemporary project for screenwriter Borden Chase, playing a modern-day engineer contracted to build either a bridge or a tunnel through a South American mountain range so an industrialist (Cedric Hardwicke) can link two disparate areas with his railroad. A forerunner of character Tom Dunson in Howard Hawks's upcoming classic *Red River*, Wayne's Johnny Munroe finds himself on the edge of a nervous breakdown owing to strains in his professional and personal life. As to the latter, Johnny wants to marry his boss's aristocratic daughter (Laraine Day), though her father disapproves. Also, as in the sprawling novel by C. E. Scoggins on which this movie is based, his inamorata's dad hopes to cut corners at every turn. "A good engineer doesn't get his men hurt," Johnny snarls at his boss's suggestion that greater risks could lead to greater profit. As in the earlier *Rainbow Valley* and John Ford's *Horse Soldiers* more than a decade later, Wayne's he-man is not some ignorant brute, but a highly educated man who has a college degree and the professional skills to put his ideas into practice. He's the new American aristocracy, achieving such status not through birth but with hard work, first at school, then in the world at large.

THE MESSAGE: No matter how much a person may enjoy making money, it is the enlightened capitalist who takes human and moral values into account to protect the humble working man and woman.

THE FIGHTIN' IRISH: In *Tycoon* Wayne played a rough fella from the wrong side of the tracks who battles his way to the top, setting the pace for his role as another rugged man of the Emerald Isle in *The Quiet Man* (seen here). *Courtesy: Republic Pictures / mptvimages.com*

ANGEL AND THE BADMAN (1947)

Director and screenwriter: James Edward Grant
"Each human being has an integrity that can be hurt only by the act of that same human being and not by the act of another human being."

As Quirt Evans, a wounded gun on the run who has taken refuge with a farming family, Wayne reads those words off a plaque in their simple home. The farmers are Quakers, a gentle religious sect Quirt learns to love, in no small part owing to a young woman (the tragic beauty Gail Russell). Initially the words fascinate but confuse Quirt. In time the phrase comes to define his personal code of conduct and encapsulates his approach to living—and loving—in a cruel world. As the producer of *Angel and the Badman*, Wayne finally was able to express himself without reporting to others. This film defines Wayne's unique brand of philosophical conservatism, which had little to do with social conservatism, as he adopted what might be called a liberal attitude on such sticky issues as movie censorship. At the end he happily lets a lawman (Harry Carey Sr.) mow down the bad guys. Quirt throws his own gun away, ready to marry and take up farming. Harry Carey smiles and says, "Only a man who carries a gun needs one"— a surprising sentiment, but one that expresses Wayne's view on the process by which a no longer relevant Wild West must necessarily give way to "civilization" and the sense of social responsibility that term implies.

THE MESSAGE: Always take full responsibility for your own actions, regardless of whether they turn out to be right or wrong. That's what rugged individualism, at its most basic and best, is actually all about.

FORT APACHE (1948)

Director: John Ford
Screenwriter: Frank S. Nugent (screenplay based on the James Warner Bellah short story "Massacre")

"I gave my word to Cochise. No man is going to make a liar out of me . . . sir!"

Here is the first, biggest, and best of Ford's cavalry trilogy starring Wayne in interlocking tales about the frontier army. Duke is cast as Capt. Kirby York, a veteran of the southwest Indian wars who must deal with a new commanding officer, Lt. Col. Owen Thursday (Henry Fonda, in a role based at least in part on George Custer). York and his sidekick sergeant (Pedro Armendáriz) are sent out to negotiate with the Apaches on a meeting place where perhaps a peace treaty can be signed. Upon returning to the title fort, York is stunned to realize that Thursday plans to use this rendezvous as a trap, surrounding the Indians in order to disarm and disable them. Furious, York barely controls his temper as he all but spits out the above words. Surprised, the arrogant commander laughs, and then answers, "There's no question of honor between an American officer and Cochise." Again treading a thin line between respect for this man's rank and an absolute insistence on maintaining personal dignity, York answers: "There is for me, sir." Here was one of the first films to treat the Native American with greater dignity, setting the pace for such pro-Indian films to come as *Broken Arrow* (1950).

THE MESSAGES: (1) Ignore ethnicity and evaluate each person who comes into your life based on their character or lack thereof. (2) Always be true to your word, which is the essence of one's personal integrity, no matter how bad the pressure may become.

PROMOTING RACIAL HARMONY: With the support of his best friend, a Mexican-American (Pedro Armendáriz), Wayne's cavalry officer attempts to negotiate a peace in *Fort Apache* with Apache leader Cochise (Miguel Inclan). *Courtesy: Al St. Hilaire / mptvimages.com*

3 GODFATHERS (1948)

Director: John Ford
Screenwriters: Laurence Stallings and Frank S. Nugent (screenplay based on a novel of the same name by Peter B. Kyne)
"They ain't payin' me to kill people."

Sheriff Perley Sweet (Ward Bond) so replies to his deputy (Hank Worden) after he seemingly misses a shot at three outlaws (Wayne, Pedro Armendáriz, and Harry Carey Jr.) who have robbed the local bank. The sheriff hit just what he was aiming at: their water bag. As no one was killed during the robbery, he has no intention of doing them in for a minor crime. "Them Texas boys are gonna be mighty thirsty before they reach water," Perley chuckles. And likely give themselves, and the money, up to deputies guarding each water hole. The title characters head off into the desert, where they promise a dying woman (Mildred Natwick) that they'll care for her newborn babe. The last surviving gang member, Robert Marmaduke Hightower (Wayne), carries the child into New Jerusalem on Christmas morning, proving that the sheriff was right in his decision to avoid bloodshed in this allegorical tale from novelist Peter B. Kyne.

THE MESSAGE: Let the punishment fit the crime. An eye for an eye and a tooth for a tooth, as the Good Book says—but only if an eye or tooth has been lost.

WAKE OF THE RED WITCH (1948)

Director: Edward Ludwig
Screenwriters: Harry Brown and Kenneth Gamet (based on the novel of the same name by Garland Roark)
"Some people don't dare to love."

Captain Ralls is hardly one of the Duke's beloved alter ego characters on the order of those encountered in *Hondo, McLintock!*, and *Chisum*. Here is a man who is described by his best friend (Gig Young) as "strange, sadistic, and cold." Not that Ralls was always so horrible. This 1860s seaman of the Dutch East Indies became a loner alcoholic after helplessly watching an unsavory businessman (Luther Adler) steal away the woman he loves (Gail Russell), and then spending his ill-fated life on a dark trail of vengeance. Think of Ralls as an odd combination of Heathcliff in Emily Brontë's *Wuthering Heights* and Wolf Larsen from Jack London's *Sea Wolf*. This salty period-noir must have had great personal meaning for John Wayne, for in time he named his own indie production unit Batjac, after the large company his character here works for, Batjak. Mostly this tale serves as a cautionary fable, with Wayne delivering one of his best performances ever as a character lead by playing an antihero whose proclivities we'd best avoid, rather than one more heroic man of action for audiences to emulate. Yet the younger Ralls's attitude about love at first sight proves truly universal.

THE MESSAGE: Although there's no way to know whether love will save you or destroy you, you still should leap at it when it comes along, because nothing else in the world—not even wealth or power—can ever come close to unconditional love.

RED RIVER (1948)

Director: Howard Hawks and Arthur Rosson
Screenwriters: Borden Chase and Charles Schnee
"You earned it!"

Hawks's inital Western offers a larger-than-life version of the first post–Civil War trek up the Chisholm Trail from Texas to Kansas. The role of Tom Dunson defies all previous misperceptions about Wayne's limited abilities as an actor. In 1951 Dunson creates a brand, the Red River "D," and emblazons it onto his own bull and onto the cow of a boy (Mickey Kuhn) who joins their small company. "My name's Matthew," the youth taunts. "I don't see an 'M' on that brand." Wayne sizes the kid up and states: "Your initial will go on that brand when you earn it."

Fifteen years later they begin the long drive, with Matt now played by Montgomery Clift. Dunson suffers a nervous breakdown, and out of necessity his adopted son takes charge and moves the herd north. At first Dunson considers this a betrayal. But when he rides into Abilene and sees (after a brief skirmish) that Matthew has indeed completed what he himself started but was unable to finish, Dunson's tune changes. "When we get back to the ranch, I want you to change the brand. Put an 'M' on it." When Matthew asks why, Dunson with a wink delivers the quote that concludes the movie.

THE MESSAGE: There are few entitlements in life. No one should expect anything other than what he proves, through deed and action, that he deserves. You get what you earn.

UP THE TRAIL FROM TEXAS: When Wayne filmed *Red River*, images of the star during the cattle drive were mostly constructed in the studio via back-projection; when Duke later headed up a drive in *The Cowboys* (seen here), on-location work was the rule of order. *Courtesy: © David Sutton / mptvimages.com*

THE FIGHTING KENTUCKIAN (1949)

Director and screenwriter: George Waggner
"This looks like a job for a hero!"

"A John Wayne Production," the credits proudly announce after the Republic studio's eagle makes an appearance. This film was one of the first examples of a star forming an independent company to co-produce with the old studios during the postwar period. The fact-based story concerns inhabitants of Demopolis ("the People's City"), Alabama, circa 1818. Former supporters of Napoleon forced to flee France following Bonaparte's fall from grace attempt to maintain their Gallic ways as a unique subculture within the multicultural scheme of America. John Breen (Duke) is a member of Andy Jackson's ragtag militia that defeated the British at New Orleans. On his way home Breen meets and falls in love with Fleurette (Vera Ralston), also the romantic target of a rich and well-suited businessman (John How-ard), who senses his lack of romantic appeal when measured against the tall man in a coonskin cap. Yet when both are held captive by bad guys (raw capitalists) who wish to steal the new settlers' land, and Duke speaks the above line, his competition for Fleurette hurries out before Breen in an ill-fated attempt to save the day. Though the fellow dies trying, John manages to reach him before his demise and, with admiration, say, "Hello, *hero.*"

THE MESSAGE: Being a hero comes down to what you do at the moment of truth. Every man can be a hero if only, as Joseph Campbell wrote, he follows his bliss.

WAYNE'S FIRST COONSKIN CAP: Nearly two decades before *The Alamo*, Wayne donned a similar costume for this 1818 frontier epic, *The Fighting Kentuckian*; here he chats with co-star Vera H. Ralston. *Courtesy: Republic Pictures / mptvimages.com*

SANDS OF IWO JIMA (1949)

Director: Allan Dwan
Screenwriters: James Edward Grant and Harry Brown
"Life is tough, but it's tougher if you're stupid."

Sgt. John Stryker (John Wayne) trains a marine platoon both state-side and in Hawaii for eventual combat in the South Pacific, with Duke playing a part that won him his only Oscar nomination prior to *True Grit*. Men under Stryker's command come to hate him for being down so hard on them. The other noncoms seem to get along great with the young volunteers, nurturing them through difficult situations relating not only to the service but also to their personal lives. Stryker pushes the boys until they think of him as a contemporary Captain Ahab.

Then comes the sheer hell of a sea-to-land campaign and, with it, a change in perception. If earlier the boys thought that Stryker's signature statement (above) revealed contempt for them, they realize, under fire, that here is the group leader who cared the most. His approach, known today by the term "tough love," gave his charges the best chances for survival. Rather than caring about his own popularity, Stryker was concerned about the safety and survival of his men. Although the grumbling trainees don't at first grasp this, their tough sergeant makes them smart, which is revealed in the way they handle themselves during the title battle. When Stryker is gone, surviving squad members come to realize just how very deeply he cared.

THE MESSAGE: True love is both tough and unconditional. No matter what anyone thinks or feels about you, if you're in command, do what you know to be best for all.

THE LONELIEST MAN ON MT. SURIBACHI: As Sergeant Stryker in *Sands of Iwo Jima*, Wayne embodies the unappreciated old warrior who must toughen up young men—little more than overgrown boys—to increase their chances of survival in combat. *Courtesy: Roman Freulich / mptvimages.com*

SHE WORE A YELLOW RIBBON (1949)

Director: John Ford
Screenwriters: Frank S. Nugent and Laurence Stallings
"The sun and moon change, but the army knows no seasons."

For many fans of the so-called Ford cavalry trilogy, the most memorable line spoken in this, the second installment (and the only one of the three to be shot in color), is "Never apologize; it's a sign of weakness." That macho mantra—spoken by Wayne's character, Capt. Nathan Brittles—means far more than it might seem to, for underneath the truly tough and seemingly callous exterior of this aging officer beats a deeply sentimental heart. This is obvious when the men award their retiring commander with a handsome gold watch (on the back, "lest we forget!" has been embossed) and Brittles can barely hold back the tears. Similar to Wayne's character in *Sands of Iwo Jima* (which was released more or less simultaneously with this Western), Captain Brittles is a true stoic in the Roman tradition: Although he tries not to show his emotions, he still experiences them. Good as that line is, this one's more important: Sergeant Quincannon (Victor McLaglen) has just said, with a sad sigh, that when these two old warhorses retire, the army will never be the same again. Far wiser, Brittles corrects his old friend: "The army is always the same . . ." Then come the above words.

THE MESSAGE: Never lose sight of your place in the universe. No matter how dedicated you are and regardless of how important your work may seem, no one person is irreplaceable.

"OLD SOLDIERS . . . : They never die . . . just fade away. Not so Capt. Nathan Brittles at film's end, though, thanks to an appealing if unlikely epilogue to *She Wore a Yellow Ribbon*, in which the veteran is called back to active duty. *Courtesy: mptvimages.com*

RIO GRANDE (1950)

Director: John Ford
Screenwriter: James Kevin McGuinness
"To my only rival, the United States Cavalry."

Kathleen Yorke (Maureen O'Hara) raises an ironic toast to the institution she competes with for the attentions of her husband, Lt. Col. Kirby Yorke (Wayne). This is not precisely the same character the Duke earlier played in *Fort Apache* (the last name has a different spelling), but a variation on that officer and all he stood for. In *Rio Grande* the husband and wife have become estranged owing to his fulfillment of an unpleasant duty: During the Civil War, Yorke, as a junior officer serving with General Sherman's infamous March to the Sea, followed orders by having his top sergeant (Victor McLaglen) burn down Yorke's Southern-born wife's beloved plantation. Even before that, however, the relationship had been strained by his absolute dedication to duty, first and foremost. On the other hand, his sense of devotion to his wife allows even her to grasp that he is completely faithful as a husband. Thus, his life is all about trying to maintain a delicate balance between the two commitments he has made.

THE MESSAGE: Sometimes the commitments one makes turn out to be contradictory, in terms of their demands on a person's time and loyalties. The most anyone can do is to honor each commitment to the best of his or her ability.

LIKE FATHER, LIKE SON: Patrick Wayne joined his dad in a handful of movies. Here, they are together in *The Searchers*, though an eleven-year-old Pat first co-starred with the Duke as "The Boy" in *Rio Grande*.
Courtesy: Warner Bros. / mptvimages.com

FLYING LEATHERNECKS (1951)

Director: Nicholas Ray
Screenwriters: James Edward Grant and Kenneth Gamet
"Take off those boots, mister!"

The Hellcats who fly missions during the battle of Guadalcanal expect that their beloved officer Capt. Carl "Griff" Griffin (Robert Ryan), who has always treated them nicely, will become the new commander of their outfit. The marines instead send in a new man: Maj. Daniel Xavier Kirby (Wayne), who quickly proves himself to be without warmth, charm, or any sort of friendliness during their daily operations. The boys resent him, and Griff even takes on Kirby in a powerful one-on-one confrontation as he sticks up for the regular fellas. There's only one problem: The way in which Griff treated the boys tended to get a lot of men killed, as they became used to a softness that isn't there in combat. Kirby toughens them up, not because he doesn't care, but, like Sgt. John Stryker in *Sands of Iwo Jima*, because he cares so very much—even about the fellow nicknamed "Cowboy" (Don Taylor), to whom he abrasively addresses the above words.

THE MESSAGE: Don't wear cowboy boots until you prove yourself on the open range—or in this case, in the wild blue yonder.

OPERATION PACIFIC (1951)

Director and screenwriter: George Waggner
"I'll never make fun of another movie as long as I live."

Duke was entirely aware that people more often than not assume that what they see in a Hollywood version of anything that occurred in life, World War II included, is only a fantasy. For that reason he wanted this epic of combat in the South Pacific to be entirely accurate. This explains why Adm. Charles A. Lockwood, who had commanded submarine activity in the area, was brought on as technical advisor. Many of the incidents in the George Waggner script actually occurred, if not in the precise manner that the story line presents here. Even Duke's character's name—Duke E. Gifford—suggests how intensely committed he was to this little-known project. The all too real problem that the servicemen face has to do with torpedoes fired at enemy ships that explode too soon and the step-by-step realization that faulty firing pins are the problem.

THE MESSAGE: As a ship's lieutenant comments above, movies do not necessarily offer an escape from reality. Rather, they can be a means of comprehending it.

AMERICAN SUPERTARS: Gary Cooper visits Wayne on the set; years later, the two hoped to co-star in *Ride the High Country* for Sam Peckinpah but Coop passed away before shooting could commence, and Duke dropped out. *Courtesy: Morgan / mptvimages.com*

BIG JIM McLAIN (1952)

Director: Edward Ludwig
Screenwriters: James Edward Grant, Richard English, and Eric Taylor
"Don't analyze it—just let it be."

In one of the least incendiary moments of this propaganda piece disguised as an action flick, Wayne as the title character says that to female lead Nancy Olson. They've met in Hawaii, where he and his G-man partner (James Arness) have arrived to track down a ring of spies and saboteurs, the heroes having been dispatched by the House Committee on Un-American Activities. A strong physical attraction blossoms into mutual respect and deep friendship. She needs to go slowly, as her late husband, who resembled Big Jim, was killed in the war. Realizing that here's the right man for the rest of her life and that there is such a thing as another chance at love, she can't help but try to understand her feelings. The Duke insists that some things are better left untouched by the mind, remaining strictly in that realm belonging to the heart. An intriguing bit of trivia: In Europe, where a Red Scare mentality did not exist, film importers sensed that such a politicized story would seem irrelevant to continental viewers. They re-created the plot without changing a frame of film, redoing the dialogue so this became a thriller about the search for drug dealers. The title in most such countries was changed to *Marijuana*.

THE MESSAGE: Most of the time it pays to test our emotional reactions via the thought process. But as Woody Allen has said, "the brain is a vastly overrated organ." Never ruin the magic of love by trying to explain it intellectually.

THE QUIET MAN (1952)

Director: John Ford
Screenwriter: Frank S. Nugent (screenplay based on a short story of
the same name by Maurice Walsh)
*"There'll be no locks or bolts between us . . . except those in your mercenary
little heart."*

Oscar nomination or (as in this case) no Oscar nomination, Sean
Thornton is John Wayne's single greatest performance, perhaps
because the man is so atypical: a former boxer who accidentally killed
an opponent in the ring and now refuses to fight anyone, under any
circumstances. This causes Sean to be mistakenly labeled a cow-
ard, at least until the final reel, when he has at it with the big-bully
brother (Victor McLaglen) of Sean's still-unravished bride (Maureen
O'Hara). As in Maurice Walsh's memorable short story, the problem
is this: Mary Kate Danaher-Thornton refuses to share her husband's
bed until she's received her full dowry, and her brother will not hand
that over until Sean fights him man-to-man. The beauty of the piece
is the manner in which Wayne's hero respects the wife's rights while
making clear that any walls between them must be invisible ones.
He allows her "privacy" but does so while insisting on an open door
policy.

*THE MESSAGE: Never violate a woman's own particular code of
honor, no matter how different hers may be from your own.*

THE GREATEST MOVIE EVER MADE ABOUT IRELAND: John Ford brought American stars Wayne and Maureen O'Hara (along with some top character actors) with him to the Emerald Isle for *The Quiet Man*, a grand tale of romance. *Courtesy: mptvimages.com*

TROUBLE ALONG THE WAY (1953)

Director: Michael Curtiz
Screenwriter: Melville Shavelson and Jack Rose
"Winning isn't everything—it's the only *thing!"*

How many generations of sports fans have believed Vince Lombardi was the first to speak that line? Apparently even that legendary light of the Green Bay Packers knew he could learn something from watching John Wayne movies. Here the words are voiced by Sherry Jackson as the daughter of Wayne's character, Steve Williams. He's a washed-up football coach who once worked at a big university until he became too greedy for victory. Accused of bringing in top athletes not enrolled as students, Steve found himself out of a job and no longer taken seriously by the major players in college ball. But if he doesn't find some job fast, he'll lose custody of his little girl. That's when Charles Coburn, as a kindly priest, comes to the rescue. You see, there's this nice little Catholic college in New York City, they'd like to improve their financial position by beefing up the sports program, and they need a talented coach who . . .

THE MESSAGE: Keep your eye on the ball, in life as in sports, until victory is yours.

ISLAND IN THE SKY (1953)

Director: William A. Wellman
Screenwriter: Ernest K. Gann

"I'll shoot the first one of you to leave camp. I'll aim at the legs. I may miss and hit you in the back of the head. Either way, serves you right."

Captain Dooley spits out those words to the frightened crew of his downed Douglas C-47 Skytrain after they make a forced landing in the wilds of Labrador during World War II. The temperatures are subzero, the food supply is pitifully low, and there's a great danger that rescue planes will not even be able to spot them in the lousy weather. Dooley knows their only chance for survival hinges on operating as a fully functioning community. Each man must depend on each of the others as someone with unique abilities he can contribute to the group. Thanks to Dooley's influence, they manage to pull together.

This was one of two films that Duke did for flying enthusiasts Wellman—who had directed the first Oscar-winning Best Picture ever, *Wings* (1927)—and Gann—who told his life story in the book *A Hostage to Fortune*. The other was *The High and the Mighty*, a big-budget item with an immense cast and sprawling length, shot in color. That rated as a prestige item, though at heart it was merely an overblown melodrama of the sort satirized in the comedy *Airplane!* *Island in the Sky*, though little more than a black-and-white B film, rates as a minor classic.

THE MESSAGE: The genius of America can be found in its delicate balance between rugged individualism and community values. As Benjamin Franklin put it, "We must all hang together, or assuredly we shall all hang separately."

HONDO (1953)

Director: John Farrow
Screenwriter: James Edward Grant (screenplay adapted from a Louis
L'Amour short story)
"A man ought to do what he thinks is right."

"Wayne's *Shane*," as more than one critic tagged this early indie produced by Wayne-Fellows Productions and distributed by Warner
Bros., was in many ways the definitive Duke vehicle. It was among
the earliest to be written specifically for him by Grant. Urban redneck
Al Bundy claimed this to be his all-time favorite film on TV's *Married with Children*. This marked the screen debut of Geraldine Page
after Katharine Hepburn backed out—Duke's desire to work with
either actress belied the myth that liberals were blacklisted from his
projects. Wayne respected both talent and a person's right to hold
ideas with which he did not personally agree. The dog, Sam (did he
really have to die, Duke?), was the son of Lassie. *Hondo* was not based
on the book of that title, which actually was written as a follow-up,
perhaps the first example of a "novelization." This is the only Wayne
film ever to be shot in 3-D process. At one point a little boy (Lee
Aaker) attempts to pet Sam. Hondo warns him against doing so, but
insists that the child, now possessing this information, should decide
for himself. The boy attempts to pet Sam anyway and gets bitten. His
mother (Page) grows furious, but Hondo will not back off from his
position.

*THE MESSAGE: Although we have an obligation to teach our youth,
sometimes they will choose to ignore our warnings and learn lessons the
hard way. We then must allow them the freedom to choose for themselves.*

FROM THE PEN OF LOUIS L'AMOUR: Wayne's role in *Hondo* was tailor-made for him by the legendary Western novelist; he poses with co-stars Lee Aaker, Geraldine Page (in her screen debut), and long-time pal/co-star Ward Bond. *Courtesy: mptvimages.com*

THE HIGH AND THE MIGHTY (1954)

Director: William A. Wellman
Screenwriter: Ernest K. Gann
"Dan Roman had the guts enough not to commit suicide."

That line is spoken about Wayne's character by an old friend (George Chandler) who knows all too well what his sad-eyed, ever whistling buddy has been through. Once a lofty captain, Dan Roman (Wayne), every bit as stoical as his name would suggest, now serves as the humble copilot of a DC-4 that's about to make what ought to be a routine flight from Honolulu to San Francisco. What Dan never talks about is an accident he inadvertently caused that took the lives of his beloved wife and son and left him with a permanent limp. No one has ever fully trusted Dan since that tragic event. Now, however, Dan has a chance to redeem himself as engine trouble develops and the young captain (Robert Stack) falls into a panic. All twenty-two lives aboard will be lost if someone doesn't rise to the occasion and become a hero. There's no better candidate for that job than a man who failed precipitously but learned from his earlier mistake.

THE MESSAGE: Everyone deserves a second chance. Just don't blow it this time around!

FAMILY FIRST! Shortly after completing the original *Airport* movie, Wayne found time to relax at home with wife Pilar and daughter Aissa.
Courtesy: © Bernie Abramson / mptvimages.com

TRACK OF THE CAT (1954)

Director: William A. Wellman
Screenwriter: A. I. Bezzerides (screenplay based on a novel of the same name by Walter Van Tilburg Clark)
"When I have fears that I may cease to be ..."

Here is another of those personal films produced by Wayne and Robert Fellows. Duke considered starring, then passed for complex reasons, allowing Robert Mitchum to assume the role of Curt Bridges, the truly rugged individualist among a high-mountain family revealed to be dysfunctional: alcoholic father, domineering mother, indecisive older brother, immature younger one, and a sad sister who, like Cassandra in ancient Ilium, can predict a tragic future but has no power to prevent it. Curt has been stealing cattle from his siblings to build up his own herd, emotionally intimidating them with his supposedly superior masculine strength and frontier prowess. Apparently, he alone can track the unseen panther (pronounced "painter") that preys on their herd during a blizzard. The film does not celebrate such a macho mentality but criticizes it. Curt's surface show of toughness dissipates once he's read the above line by poet John Keats. He panics, he dies (not by the panther's claws but from his own long-hidden fears), he is replaced by a true hero—a boy name Tab Hunter (Harold Bridges)—who proves his manhood through humility and a quiet self-confidence.

THE MESSAGE: The only man who need fear his death is the one who knows, deep inside, that he has not lived his life as he ought to have.

BLOOD ALLEY (1955)

Director: William A. Wellman
Screenwriter: Albert Sidney Fleischman
"If you want a last look at home, you'd better take it now."

The Duke never chose to remain quiet about his political positions. Some of them, like his love of people from diverse ethnicities and his concern about the environment, may in retrospect make him appear something of a liberal. In his time, though, Wayne was known as "Mr. Conservative," and the issue that absolutely qualified him for that status was a hatred of communism. Whenever possible, he tried to incorporate that into the movies that he made during the postwar years, always careful to keep any didacticism secondary to the big, splashy entertainment values. Here he's a merchant marine officer who takes on the responsibility of using a creaky old ship that can barely stay afloat to transport an entire village of anticommunist Chinese off to safety (and political freedom) in Hong Kong. As they leave, he takes a good friend (Henry Nakamura) to the stern and tells him to never forget what happened here, and why.

THE MESSAGE: Don't look back, Bob Dylan warned in the mid-1960s. Wayne would offer us precisely the opposite advice. Always take one final glance backward to remember what you're leaving behind.

WAYNE VS. THE REDS: During the Cold War, the Duke appeared in patriotic films even as he had in World War II; in *Blood Alley*, he and Lauren Bacall help refugees escape from the encroaching Red Chinese by boat. *Courtesy: mptvimages.com*

THE SEA CHASE (1955)

Director: John Farrow
Screenwriters: James Warner Bellah and John Twist (screenplay based
on a novel of the same name by Andrew Geer)
"Don't confuse sincerity of purpose with success."

During the postwar years international alliances changed and changed
fast. Whereas during the great crusade in Europe, America and Rus-
sia had aligned to fight Germany, in the reconfigured cold war era the
Soviet Union emerged as our great antagonist, while a humbled Germany had to be accepted as an important ally. Hollywood did its share
to help the public adjust to and accept this drastic realignment by making films that depicted as heroic figures those Germans who had fer-
vently opposed the Nazi party and the fascist political philosophy. As
the fact-based Karl Ehrlich, Wayne embodied just such a person, as the
lead character attempts to navigate his aged freighter from Australia to
Germany, past the Allied fleet. As a German, he wants to go home; as
an anti-Nazi, he is deeply ashamed of the moral depths to which his
homeland has sunk. Adding to the drama in this adaptation of a novel
by Andrew Geer is that a Nazi agent (Lyle Bettger) aboard the boat
frames Erhlich for atrocities he himself committed. In this project the
Duke had an opportunity to play a man dealing with a complex two-
way stretch that offers no easy way out other than to stick to his guns
and travel full speed ahead, hoping for the best while fearing the worst.

*THE MESSAGE: Every individual must face profound moral choices
in an imperfect world that competes for our allegiance. Regardless of outside pressures, the highest allegiance should be to your personal values, no
matter how insurmountable the odds may be.*

THE SEARCHERS (1956)

Director: John Ford
Screenwriter: Frank S. Nugent (screenplay adapted from the novel of the same name by Alan Le May)
"That'll be the day!"

Perhaps the single most memorable film among the many classics John Wayne starred in for John Ford, *The Searchers* tells a tale at once epic and tragic. When two young women are abducted by Comanches following an 1867 massacre, their uncle, Ethan Edwards (Wayne), and the family's unofficially adopted son, Martin Pawley (Jeffrey Hunter), set out on a five-year quest to find the lone surviving girl. Young Marty, himself part Native American, worries whether Ethan plans to kill little Debbie (Lana Wood in early sequences, her sister Natalie later) owing to this complex man's deep-seated racism. Martin finally helps Ethan not only leave behind his hatred, but also accept his niece despite her marriage to an Indian.

Throughout the film Martin continues to remain sure of their eventual success. Ethan's reply, quoted above, appears five different times—each time in a unique way that's best suited to the current situation.

THE MESSAGE: Idealism may seem like the best approach, but if you always expect the worst, you will seldom be disappointed.

"THEY HAD TO FIND HER . . .": In *The Searchers*, Wayne and Jeff Hunter as Ethan Edwards and Martin Pawley set out on a five-year quest to find a stolen child; few films, even others by Ford, so fully capture the epic grandeur of Monument Valley as this classic. *Courtesy: Warner Bros. / mptvimages.com*

THE CONQUEROR (1956)

Director: Dick Powell
Screenwriter: Oscar Millard
"Before the sun sets, you will come willingly to my arms."

According to John Wayne himself, the true message of this film was that a star should never "make an ass of yourself trying to play parts you're not suited for." He was referring, of course, to his miscasting as Temujin, later Genghis Khan, supreme commander of the Mongol hordes. On a far more serious note, in fact a tragic one, another message would be: Never shoot a film on a location that was recently employed as a nuclear weapon testing site; virtually everyone in the cast and crew of this RKO spectacular eventually died of cancer, likely contracted while working on the Nevada desert. As to the film itself, Temujin falls in love at first sight with Bortai (Susan Hayward), daughter of a Tartar leader. He kidnaps the princess and brings her to his camp, leaving no doubt in her mind as to what he wants. Like the Maureen O'Hara character in a contemporary or period picture, this other redhead knows that however many lands (and the men in it) this mighty man may conquer, he falls apart at the seams every time he looks at her. She will continue to be his captive, no question about that, perhaps even in a forced marriage. But as was the case in the far more successful film *The Quiet Man*, he will not lay a hand on this beautiful object of his desire until she decides that she wants him to. And in due time, and after much frustration for our hero, that is of course precisely what does transpire.

THE MESSAGE: The greatest respect a man can show to a woman is to give her freedom of choice. Offer her that, and in time she will love you for it—even if you're a barbarian!

A CAMP CLASSIC: In later years, John Wayne took to good-naturedly kidding himself (particularly that eye makeup!) for having essayed the role of Genghis Khan, ancient conqueror of more than half the world. *Courtesy: mptvimages.com*

SEVEN MEN FROM NOW (1956)

Director: Budd Boetticher
Screenwriter: Burt Kennedy
"A man ought to be able to take care of his woman."

If only the Duke had starred as Ben Stride in this pluperfect B Western, produced by Wayne (uncredited) and Batjac, rather than as Ghengis Khan in *The Conqueror*! But as Wayne's schedule proved too busy, Duke offered old saddle pal Randolph Scott what proved to be the role of a lifetime. Stride, identified as a small-town sheriff, sets out to track down seven men who, during a Wells Fargo robbery, killed his wife, a clerk for that company's local office. But all is not as it seems. Taken at face value, the above line might be thought of as an example of macho posturing on the part of an embittered man out to prove just how tough he is. In fact, the character—as written for Wayne and played by Scott—is actually expressing his deep self-doubts and concern about his worth as a person. The reason our antihero's wife happened to be working that night was that he'd been fired. We are never told what his weakness was—alcohol, most likely—but the effect is even more powerful for our not knowing the specifics. He failed to live up to his end of the bargain that is marriage; he, not the outlaws, is responsible. What Ben Stride wants is less vengeance than redemption.

THE MESSAGE: Being a man has less to do with your profession than with being a total professional at whatever job you have. Always take personal responsibility for your own failures.

GUN THE MAN DOWN (1956)

Director: Andrew V. McLaglen
Screenwriters: Sam Freedle and Burt Kennedy
"Explain? You mean there's a reason to run off and leave a man to the posse? There's an explanation for that?"

Though hardly a classic B movie like *Seven Men from Now*, this sturdy low-budgeter from Batjac has several things going for it. Wayne employed this small project as a test run for several performers, including Angie Dickinson (Janice), who would play the female lead in *Rio Bravo* three years later. Kennedy and McLaglen would both regularly work with Batjac in the 1960s. Most impressive, though, is James Arness, whom Wayne had begun to groom for stardom as a younger version of himself. Arness's character of Rem Anderson certainly recalls the roles young Wayne played: a wounded outlaw who, after a botched bank robbery, is left behind by his two partners and his girl. He ends up in jail while they go off with the loot. Once released, Rem heads out on the vengeance trail to teach the trio a lesson. In fact, he's the one who gets an education when he confronts Janice and shouts the above into her face. Yes, there is! She wanted him to acquire his ranch by working for it, not becoming a bandit. Moreover, she didn't choose to leave Rem, but was physically forced to while he was unconscious. He finally realizes that what seemed clear to him turned out to be more complex than he had thought.

THE MESSAGE: Vengeance is easy, but most easy things require little intelligence. The wise man will take into account another's perspective before jumping to conclusions.

THE WINGS OF EAGLES (1957)

Director: John Ford
Screenwriters: Frank Fenton and William Wister Haines (screenplay based on a book of the same name by Frank Wead)
"I'm gonna move that toe!"

In what may be the Duke's most underappreciated performance, he—playing the real-life aviation pioneer Frank W. "Spig" Wead (1895–1947)—speaks that line after his neck has been broken in a household accident. No one expects him to regain any control over his body again. Another person might have shrugged and accepted that cruel trick of fate. "There goes the rest of my life" could be the expected response to such a tragedy, which was particularly potent because Wead had been a pioneer of American aviation. But Wead, ever the good soldier, realized that although he might have had to reduce the size of the challenges he set, that didn't mean he ought to stop pushing himself to the limit.

Wead went on to write some of the most accurate and enthralling motion pictures ever made on the subject of aviation, including *Test Pilot*, *Dive Bomber*, and *Hell Divers*. *They Were Expendable*, his script for John Ford (played by Ward Bond in *The Wings of Eagles*), about servicemen stuck on Corregidor at the beginning of World War II, resulted in a true American classic. Both in life and on-screen, Wead insisted on creating his own fate, rather than leaving his situation in the hands of others. Wead seized control of what remained of his life, making it rewarding. Who better to play him than the star whose own personal code followed the same set of rules?

THE MESSAGE: A man's only limitations are those that he sets for himself in his mind.

LEGEND OF THE LOST (1957)

Director: Henry Hathaway
Screenwriters: Ben Hecht and Robert Presnell Jr.
"You live your way, and I'll live mine!"

Released within months of *The Wings of Eagles* (fabulous!) and not that long after *The Conqueror* (not so much), *Legend of the Lost* made clear that Duke was interested in a change of pace at this point in his career. He set aside his adored Westerns, World War II epics, and contemporary actioners to try different things. Here he's cast in a role like the ones Humphrey Bogart so often played. Joe January, an expatriate living in Timbuktu (the film was shot near Tripoli), is hired to take Paul Bonnard (Rossano Brazzi), a civilized European dude, and his companion (Sophia Loren, who plays a mystery woman) into the Sahara to search for hidden treasure in a lost city. Before they shove off, Bonnard tells his world-weary guide that he's opposed to the liquor January is packing. "Well, I'm not," January answers. "We'll compromise." Bonnard, realizing January will not budge on this one, agrees to accept the situation by pretending those bottles are filled with some sort of medicine. "Best desert remedy on the market," January says with a smile. And off they go!

THE MESSAGE: When the heck did "compromise" become a dirty word? A perfect world in which you always have your own way will never be more than a fantasy.

THE MAN IN THE HAT: Long before George Lucas and Steven Spielberg gave their old-fashioned hero Indiana Jones a signature hat, Wayne had one; he wore it in *Legend of the Lost* and, seen here, an ad for a popular brewery. *Courtesy: © Paul Hesse / mptvimages.com*

TIME OFF FOR GOOD BEHAVIOR: Never one to favor the glitz and glamour of Hollywood, Wayne most enjoyed spending his time off in his home on Louise St. in Encino, California. *Courtesy: © Bernie Abramson / mptvimages.com*

JET PILOT (1957)

Directors: Josef von Sternberg and Jules Furthman
Screenwriters: Jules Furthman and Howard Hughes
"I could learn a few things from you."

Col. Jim Shannon (Wayne) says that to Anna (Janet Leigh) after she, a Russian pilot, lands her jet at an arctic base. Shortly, Anna is flying alongside Shannon, claiming to have picked up great moves from her new mentor. Here, as always, Duke's character knows better than to underestimate a female. Upon Anna's arrival at the base, two other air force guys gasp, "A lady" and "A dame." Wayne, ahead of his time in terms of men addressing females properly, is enlightened enough to say, "A woman!" When a general grouses, "I can't get used to women soldiers," Shannon sets him straight as to how effective a "she" can be. Anna is actually Olga, a Russian spy sent to seduce Shannon and gather info about the U.S. Air Force. He turns the tables on her. Wayne agreed to do this film for producer Howard Hughes in the early 1950s because of their mutual love of aviation and hatred for communism. Little did the star realize that Hughes's bizarre approach to moviemaking would keep him busy, on and off, for nearly three years, with Hughes then spending another four years editing and re-editing a movie that had been intended as an up-to-date educational film about aerial strategy, but ended up as a badly dated relic from an earlier era.

THE MESSAGE: The female of the species is often deadlier than the male. Never be fool enough to underestimate the potential of a female, be she your adversary or ally.

THE BARBARIAN AND THE GEISHA (1958)

Director: John Huston
Screenwriters: Charles Grayson and Ellis St. Joseph
"No one stays as he was, or any country."

At the height of his stardom, John Wayne could now pick and choose among projects, doing only those with great appeal to him personally. The historical figure Townsend Harris piqued Duke's interest, and he agreed to play the role in a biographical film. In 1856 Harris followed Commodore Matthew Perry's lead, arriving in Japan to serve as the United States' first consul general to that nation. Harris was met by fierce resistance after landing in the seaport town of Shimoda. The local governor (Sô Yamamura) explained that since their earlier negotiations with Perry—during which the commodore, like Harris, was following orders from President Franklin Pierce—a combination of local crop failures and terrible storms that devastated the area caused the citizenry to believe their gods were warning them against joining the then evolving international community of nations. Townsend's chief task was to convince first the governor and then the country's leadership that these were coincidences and natural phenomena, not direct messages from the divine. With James Edward Grant on board to "Duke the script up" a bit, adding lines of dialogue more in line with Wayne's persona than with anything attributed to Townsend per historical records, this version of the tale offers a progressive view that applies to where our country was in 1958 as well.

THE MESSAGE: However threatening it may seem, change not only is inevitable, but more often than not can be for the good.

THE HORSE SOLDIERS (1959)

Director: John Ford
Screenwriters: John Lee Mahin and Martin Rackin (screenplay based on a novel of the same name by Harold Sinclair)
"I didn't want this. I tried to avoid a fight."

Col. John Marlowe (Wayne) inadvertently shouts that out during the Battle of Newton's Station, an actual 1863 incident from the Civil War, in this fictionalized but overall historically accurate retelling of the Grierson Raid. In 1863 Col. Benjamin Grierson of the Union army headed south with some seventeen hundred men to destroy the railroad ties so essential to Confederate communications and troop movements. In so doing, Grierson, here reimagined in the character of Marlowe to better suit Wayne's persona, hoped to end the war quickly . . . and bloodlessly! The midpoint battle with desperate but indomitable Johnny Rebs was an unavoidable and regrettable incident. Here then is evidence to disprove the myth that the Duke's films are exercises in glorifying war. Like all the other war films in which Wayne appeared, his films are as anti-war as they are positive portrayals of those who must fight them. When Marlowe is accused by another officer (William Holden) of failing to play by the rules, Marlowe reminds the fellow: "War isn't exactly a civilized business."

THE MESSAGE: War is hell, and don't let anyone tell you otherwise. That doesn't mean we can't revere the men who volunteer to do the fighting when—the human race being imperfect at best—all other options have been exhausted.

TAKING THINGS IN STRIDE: By the late 1950s, it was clear to all that John Wayne, relaxing here on the set, now fully embodied the ideal of the traditional American male. *Courtesy: mptvimages.com*

RIO BRAVO (1959)

Director: Howard Hawks
Screenwriters: Jules Furthman and Leigh Brackett (screenplay based on a short story by B. H. McCampbell)
"'Sorry' don't get it done."

Throughout this virtual remake of and dramatic alternative to *High Noon* (1953), John T. Chance (Wayne) attempts to help his former deputy, Dude (Dean Martin in a role originally intended for Montgomery Clift), clean up his act. Long ago Dude was the best man around the town that lends this film its title. But a certain kind of woman wandered in, tore the tough guy apart at his very seams, and then left him drowning in a pool of booze. When a land baron (John Russell) threatens the town, Chance tries to get Dude in shape to help him take on the virtual army riding their way. But no matter how hard Dude tries, he eventually reaches for the bottle, and then offers his apologies, insisting that he's too weak to reform. Thankfully, the Duke knows better.

THE MESSAGE: You're as strong as you tell yourself that you're going to be, so it's up to you to stand up and take command of your own life.

THERE'S THAT HAT AGAIN! As Sheriff John T. Chance, Duke continued his ongoing persona in *Rio Bravo* by wearing the battered hat that had become his favorite. *Courtesy: mptvimages.com*

THE ALAMO (1960)

Director: John Wayne
Screenwriter: James Edward Grant
"Republic. I like the sound of the word! Means people can live free, talk free, go or come, buy or sell . . . however they choose."

Ostensibly, Davy Crockett says these lines in John Wayne's most ambitious and highly personal project. Likely, though, had the Duke played Jim Bowie or Sam Houston, it would have been Wayne who spoke them in the film's context. Indeed this quote defines John Wayne's overarching philosophy on life. In fact, Wayne considered this speech so important that he made certain it was included on the movie's soundtrack album, along with Dimitri Tiomkin's brilliant musical score—arguably the greatest ever composed for any Hollywood film. However much Wayne was called conservative or Republican, if any label fits at all, it would have to be *"libertarian."* Here was the first Alamo movie to dare to be pro-Mexican, making clear that Latinos not only attacked the fort-mission, but aided in its defense. The contributions of women and African Americans to the cause of freedom are also emphasized. Seems like *The Alamo* was the first film to support today's idea of "diversity," long before that term was created.

THE MESSAGE: America's most admirable attribute is its promise of absolute freedom for every individual to make choices according to his or her own unique sensibilities.

ONE MAN'S VISION: Though friends suggested he ought to hire Ford, Hawks, or Walsh for the job, John Wayne considered *The Alamo* his most personal project and insisted on directing it himself.
Courtesy: mptvimages.com

NORTH TO ALASKA (1960)

Director: Henry Hathaway
Screenwriters: John Lee Mahin, Martin Rackin, and Claude Binyon
"It's my only politics: anti-marriage! Any woman who devotes herself to making one man miserable instead of a lot of men happy don't get my vote."

In one of several films and TV shows designed to capitalize on Alaska's becoming our forty-ninth state in 1958, Sam McCord (Wayne) and his partner George Pratt (Stewart Granger) discover their gold mine. Sam then heads back to Seattle to pick up George's fiancée and bring her up north for marriage, only to learn she's already spoken for. Instead he persuades Angel (Capucine), a prostitute, to come along on the boat trip. Only problem is, she thinks Sam wants her for himself.

Anyone searching for an in-film quote to try to prove that the Duke was a misogynist will seize on this one—although a closer examination, particularly of its context, proves the opposite. If anything, the sentiment is anti-marriage, not anti-woman. It's worth noting that many radical feminists of the 1970s insisted that marriage was an outdated institution. More correctly, the film is a fighting doctrine for women's rights, attacking dichotomization of women.

While in Seattle, Sam takes Angel as his date to a picnic. A puritanical married woman (Kathleen Freeman) scolds Sam, who furiously responds that every woman ought to be judged as an individual person, not according to her profession. Sam treats Angel with the greatest respect. Though George is initially resentful of Angel, he's gradually won over by her warmth and decency as a person even more than by her beauty. Even George's little brother Billy (Fabian) woos her. At the end Sam puts his anti-marriage vow aside to ask for Angel's hand, even managing to say the toughest words for a he-man: "I love you!"

THE MESSAGE: Never measure the worth of a woman by her past, including her relationships with other men. It's the person inside that counts.

THE COMANCHEROS (1961)

Directors: Michael Curtiz and John Wayne
Screenwriters: James Edward Grant and Clair Huffaker (screenplay based on a novel of the same name by Paul Wellman)
"Words are what men live by. Words? They 'say.' And 'mean'!"

Following the ambitiousness of *The Alamo*, superstar Wayne glided through several big-scale though less didactic projects. *The Comancheros* concerns a tough Texas Ranger, Jake Cutter, whose assignment is to pick up Paul Regret (Stuart Whitman), a gambler who fled New Orleans because of a trumped-up murder charge. Problem is, Regret saves Jake's life, giving this film's variation on the Wayne persona reason to pause. Part of Jake wants to turn his back and let Regret slip away, particularly after it becomes clear to Jake that the man Regret killed had it coming. But since Jake took an oath, he can't do what his heart requests. Here is where, even in a film clearly designed for fun and frolic, Wayne and Grant can't help slipping in something serious: the code of personal conduct that defined Wayne.

Too often people perceive Wayne as a man of action, perhaps contemptuous of speech. The following year, in *The Man Who Shot Liberty Valance*, his character complains to Jimmy Stewart's easterner character: "You talk too much, think too much!" Nevertheless, it becomes clear that Stewart's loquacious character is a man of honesty and integrity.

THE MESSAGE: Some people believe you are what you eat, but the truth is, you are what you say. A person is only as good as his or her word.

THE DIRECTOR'S CHAIR: Wayne's experience directing *The Alamo* (seen here) came in handy when Michael Curtiz became ill on *The Comancheros* set, leaving Duke to take over; he was too much of a gentleman to take screen credit, leaving that solely to Curtiz. *Courtesy: Batjac / mptvimages.com*

THE MAN WHO SHOT LIBERTY VALANCE (1962)

Director: John Ford
Screenwriters: James Warner Bellah and Willis Goldbeck (screenplay based on a story of the same name by Dorothy M. Johnson)
"When the legend becomes fact, print the legend."

Revisionism in the Western genre began with this iconic film, even in the landscape: Gone are the starkly gorgeous Monument Valley settings, replaced by a dreary midwestern prairie.

Wayne plays Tom Doniphon, a cowboy on the fading frontier. Into the unglamorous town of Shinbone comes a man from the East, Ransom Stoddard (James Stewart). Doniphon notices pretty quickly that Ranse is a man of the future, while he himself is a relic of the past. But without Tom's guidance Ranse could never learn to use a gun and kill off the meanest outlaw of all, Liberty Valance (Lee Marvin), in an after-midnight street shootout. Or did he?

Years later Ranse and his wife (Vera Miles) return to the town. A newspaperman (Carleton Young) asks what really happened way back then. Eager to at last set the record straight, Ranse admits that Tom, unbeknownst to him at the time, plugged Liberty with a rifle from an alley. But instead of printing that story, the journalist tears it up while speaking the words quoted above.

THE MESSAGE: Perhaps there is no such thing as "the truth," only a series of truths that in time supplant one another. If not an endorsement of revisionism, Ford and Wayne here vividly illustrated how and why that process would shortly occur. We do need to believe in heroes, even if, truth be told, they are never quite able to live up to their reputations.

THE TOWN TAMER: Though James Stewart's character makes his reputation by supposedly killing the title character (Lee Marvin), the Duke's character really did it; here he takes on Lee Van Cleef and Strother Martin. *Courtesy: mptvimages.com*

THE LONGEST DAY (1962)

Directors: Ken Annakin, Andrew Marton, and Bernhard Wicki
Screenwriters: Cornelius Ryan and James Jones
"Cut those boys down! Don't leave 'em hangin' there."

Darryl F. Zanuck, head honcho at 20th Century Fox, reinvented the World War II film by adapting a docudrama approach. The massive D-Day invasion (June 6, 1944) is re-created from multiple points of view (Allied, Axis, and the French citizenry) to allow audiences a comprehensive overview. To ensure that moviegoers did not become confused, Zanuck chose major stars for various historical roles. Wayne plays Lt. Col. Benjamin Vandervoort, commanding airborne outfits that parachute inland as other crack divisions attack the coastline in land-to-sea operations. In a terrible error the paratroopers, set to drift down into the woods outside of Sainte-Mère-Église, instead find themselves falling into the city center. There they prove easy targets for German soldiers. When Vandervoort arrives, to his dismay, the dead bodies of brave men hang all around the city, their parachutes caught on high steeple towers.

More often than not cast as a stoic who keeps his emotions to himself, Wayne can indeed reveal deep feelings—particularly for those who fought bravely and died unnecessarily—and here (as well as elsewhere in his film canon) barely holds back tears.

THE MESSAGE: Although sentimentality should be avoided at all costs, sensitivity allows for emotional responses to human tragedy. Don't let anyone tell you that real men don't cry.

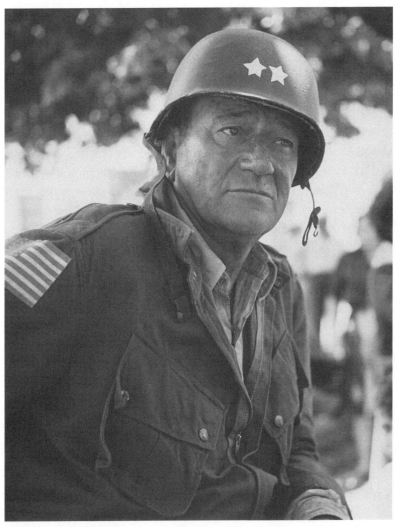

GETTIN' THE JOB DONE: Wayne joined dozens of other stars as part of Darryl F. Zanuck's ensemble for that Hollywood giant's last hurrah to a bygone age of heroes and old-fashioned moviemaking.
Courtesy: © David Sutton / mptvimages.com

HOW THE WEST WAS WON (1962)

Director: John Ford (Civil War sequence only)
Screenwriters: James R. Webb and John Gay
"'Hero' or 'crazy,' I'm the same man."

This Cinerama-lensed epic offered a sprawling attempt to create an apotheosis of the old-fashioned Western at precisely that juncture when the time-tested genre was slipping into a period of decline. Though Ford is credited with directing the Civil War sequence, the battle scenes are actually stock footage from *Raintree County* (1958). However, Ford did indeed shoot the sequence in which a down-hearted Gen. U. S. Grant (Harry Morgan) has a heart-to-heart with his field commander, Gen. William Tecumseh Sherman (Wayne). With the press coming down on him hard owing to major defeats, Grant admits he's considering retiring as commander of all Union forces. "A man only has the right to quit when he was wrong," Sherman insists, knowing that Grant's decisions were sound if not always successful. Sherman also mentions that the newspapers have ruthlessly attacked him as well, though they did a turnabout when several of his own strategies worked out for the best. Understanding the power of the press to shape naïve minds, Sherman insists: "It doesn't matter what the people think . . . it's what *you* think." In this version of the Battle of Shiloh, Grant is inspired by this small but pungent speech to "go ahead," as David Crockett would say.

THE MESSAGE: Never bow to popular opinion, which more often than not turns out to be dead wrong. As Owen Thursday (Henry Fonda) told Kirby York (John Wayne) in **Fort Apache**, *"When you're in command . . .* command!"

TOUGH GUYS, TOGETHER AGAIN: Wayne and Richard Widmark clicked as a team in *The Alamo* (seen here); two years later both would appear in *How the West Was Won*, a sprawling Cinerama epic, this time not sharing any scenes.   *Courtesy: Batjac / United Artists / mptvimages.com*

HATARI! (1962)

Director: Howard Hawks
Screenwriter: Leigh Brackett
"First sign of spring in the bush, and the young bucks start butting heads."

Sean Mercer heads up a band of trackers who capture animals in East Africa for zoos all over the world. There could not be a more diverse group than this, which contains women and men of every ethnicity. What each has in common is a keen professionalism, tying a loose coalition of rugged individualists into a tight community, every member totally relying on each other. This is a key Hawks theme also present in *Rio Bravo*, which was likewise written by Leigh Brackett, a scriptwriter who understood the incendiary chemistry present when macho men meet strong, smart women and sense their equality (perhaps superiority!). Duke's words after observing the fellas going gaga over the remarkable young women—each as brainy as she is beautiful—reveal a humorous, down-to-earth admission that nature's strong pull can be difficult to resist, regardless of how much turmoil it can cause.

THE MESSAGE: Sex is an innate part of life. Don't let anyone tell you there's anything wrong with experiencing natural human attraction.

McLINTOCK! (1963)

Director: Andrew V. McLaglen
Screenwriter: James Edward Grant
"I haven't lost my temper in forty years, but Pilgrim, you caused a lot of trouble this morning . . ."

This is the only film other than *Liberty Valance* in which Wayne refers to another character as "Pilgrim." In that movie, this served as a term of endearment to a well-meaning if unrealistic dude. Here the word is spoken harshly to a troublemaker (Leo V. Gordon) trying to stir up violence between the cowboy element and recently arrived sodbusters. As cattle baron George Washington McLintock, Wayne—perhaps surprisingly—isn't a spokesperson for conservative resistance to all change, but the mediator who believes progress should and must be embraced.

Grant tailored the piece specifically for Wayne's now firmly established persona and the person who stood tall behind it. While McLintock employs violence only as the last resort, he will use it when absolutely necessary. That includes an open threat to a cavalry sergeant caught bullying a Native American whom McLintock respects and admires, despite their combat back in the bad old days. In the rough-hewn diversity of the evolving West McLintock and a Jewish businessman (Jack Kruschen) mentor a young Native American to embrace the work ethic he needs to achieve the American dream.

THE MESSAGE: When the government's one-size-fits-all approach doesn't work, it's best to bring in someone who will take the time to understand and accommodate all points of view.

A FAMILY AFFAIR: Wayne carefully balanced career with family values; daughter Aissa was three when she appeared in *The Alamo* (seen here), six when she played a pioneer child in *McLintock!*. *Courtesy: Batjac / mptvimages.com*

DONOVAN'S REEF (1963)

Director: John Ford
Screenwriters: Frank S. Nugent and James Edward Grant
"Frangipani and flamethrowers don't seem to go together, but that's the way it was."

Imagine *McLintock!* remade as a non-Western, filmed on the isle of Kauai at Christmas, with some Howard Hawks–style good-natured brawling between top-billed male stars Wayne and Lee Marvin, and anyone who hasn't seen this grand entertainment will sense the genial fun to be found here. Elizabeth Allen as Amelia plays a spoiled Boston society matron who arrives in this paradise with plans of bringing the locals "up" to her level. Finally letting her hair down, she falls in love with big brute Michael Patrick Donovan (Wayne). Donovan takes some time out from winning her hand to attack her long-standing prejudices and win her over to his own more progressive views. Amelia finally realizes that the "simple" natives are more in tune with nature and God than self-important Anglos and that racial bigotry is stupid and wrong.

Despite an easygoing sensibility, *Donovan's Reef* is no escapist fare. The film comes out in favor of mixed ethnic marriages and against corporate greed. The Duke speaks the above quote when Amelia has trouble grasping that World War II occurred not so long ago in this rediscovered Eden. Frangipani, by the way, is a shrub with gorgeous flowers sprouting along its rough yet elegant limbs.

THE MESSAGE: Beware of being lured into complacency by the apparent beauty of your surroundings, and never take peace and prosperity for granted.

CIRCUS WORLD (1964)

Director: Henry Hathaway
Screenwriters: Ben Hecht, James Edward Grant, Julian Zimet, Bernard Gordon, Philip Yordan, and Nicholas Ray
"When a fellow's out of work, he gets himself a job."

Circus World was shot in Super Technirama 70, a process similar to Cinerama minus those off-putting vertical lines that divided the long screen into three parts. At the turn of the century, Matt Masters suddenly tells his partner and best pal (Lloyd Nolan) that he has decided to take his combination circus and Wild West show to Europe. On the very night that their immense ship docks in Barcelona, everything goes wrong that can, beginning with the great boat overturning. Almost everything is lost. Matt sinks from multimillionaire to pauper in a moment. Sound familiar? That's not a far cry from what happened to the Duke when *The Alamo* failed to bring in the hoped-for box office returns. So the above line fits not only Masters but the actor playing him—one more example of an autobiographical undercurrent to John Wayne's projects. Anyway, Matt returns to his humble beginnings, taking a job with a show that belongs to his one-time competitor. In due time he puts together enough money to get started toward the big time all over again—just as Wayne himself did, taking roles in other people's movies during the early 1960s . . . including this one.

THE MESSAGE: If life throws lemons at you, make lemonade, sell it, and use the profits to begin your life's journey once again.

IN HARM'S WAY (1965)

Director: Otto Preminger
Screenwriter: Wendell Mayes (screenplay based on the novel *Harm's Way* by James Bassett)
"Fish, or cut bait. Get on your feet, or take your troubles elsewhere. I've got a ship to run."

Shortly after the Japanese sneak attack on Pearl Harbor, Capt. Rockwell "Rock" Torrey (Wayne) is doing his best to harass the enemy with one of the few remaining American ships, a heavy cruiser. Plans for battle are hampered by the sad state of his friend, Cmdr. Paul Eddington (Kirk Douglas). Once a trusted naval career officer, Paul has fallen into chronic alcoholism as a result of the death, during the December 7 attack, of his wife (Barbara Bouchet), a shameless flirt who was having an affair with another officer (Hugh O'Brian). Paul wants Rock to cut him some slack, but Rock will have none of it. Rock refuses enable Paul to slip deeper into his self-pity—the very state of mind that he must overcome if he is to rebuild his life. Though Rock may seem insensitive, he grasps that nothing would worsen the situation more than codependency. As Humphrey Bogart famously told Ingrid Bergman at the end of *Casablanca*, the problems we little people face must be seen as pretty small potatoes in a world on the brink of ruination.

THE MESSAGE: "When the going gets tough," Joseph Kennedy once famously stated, "the tough get going." The best possible medicine for the suffering individual is to stop focusing on one's own problems and do what you can to help others.

THE GREATEST STORY EVER TOLD (1965)

Directors: George Stevens, David Lean (uncredited), and Jean Negulesco (uncredited)
Screenwriters: George Stevens, Henry Denker, Fulton Oursler, and James Lee Barrett
"Truly, he is the Son of God."

Following the commercial and critical disaster of *The Conqueror*, Wayne steadfastly insisted that he would never again appear in a movie about the ancient world. Less than ten years later he reneged when director George Stevens, famous for such classics as *Shane* (1953) and *Giant* (1956), invited the Duke to join an all-star cast (listed in alphabetical order, quite the fashion for mid-1960s spectacles) for this version of the life of Christ. Whereas earlier Hollywood versions such as Nicholas Ray's then recent *King of Kings* (1961) allowed Jesus to remain a distant figure, focusing on action/romance for the supporting characters, Stevens kept Jesus front and center. Swedish superstar Max von Sydow was picked to play a notably untypical Jesus, so far as centuries of culture go, sporting a Beatle-like haircut and revealing a smart sense of humor as well as the expected spirituality. At film's end, when the crucifixion occurs, a tall, rugged Roman centurion (Duke) quietly stands vigil, watching the events objectively and unable owing to his station to interfere. But when the skies darken and nature appears to rebel against this gross injustice, he speaks the film's final judgment.

THE MESSAGE: Seeing is believing.

EYEWITNESS TO HISTORY: As Max von Sydow, certainly an offbeat choice to play Jesus, ascends to Golgotha in *The Greatest Story Ever Told,* Wayne follows as the Centurion, representing the common man and his reactions to the crucifixion.   *Courtesy: Floyd McCarty / mptvimages.com*

THE SONS OF KATIE ELDER (1965)

Director: Henry Hathaway
Screenwriters: William H. Wright, Allan Weiss, Harry Essex, and Talbot Jennings
"All we want to do is make you rich and respectable."

The oldest of the Elder brothers, John (Wayne), speaks these words in frustration to the youngest, Bud (Michael Anderson Jr.). The four brothers, having gone their separate ways long ago, return to their Texas cow town after learning that their mother passed away in poverty. The boys (including Dean Martin and Earl Holliman), having left the widowed lady to fend for herself, now want to redeem themselves. John, a gunfighter, decides the best way to make up for their past sins would be to take back the lucrative Elder ranch from the gunsmith (James Gregory) who stole it from the family in a fixed card game, then employ the profits to send young Bud to college. This will provide a means to the end that John expresses in the above quote. Although Bud dreams of becoming an adventurer like his brothers, he finally realizes the days of the Wild West are numbered. Though many devout fans never realized this, and Duke himself didn't mention it much, he was college educated and proud of it.

THE MESSAGE: As country star Kris Kristofferson (himself a Rhodes Scholar) put it, "Freedom is just another word for nothing left to lose." In our "land of opportunity," a college education can help ensure the financial freedom needed to advance in our capitalist system and live out the American dream.

CAST A GIANT SHADOW (1966)

Director and screenwriter: Melville Shavelson (screenplay based on a book of the same name by Ted Berkman)
"L'Chaim!"

As Gen. Mike Randolph, a Patton-like character, Wayne raises a glass, offering that oldest of Hebrew toasts, "To life!" One of the most insidious myths about the Duke is that he was an anti-Semite. Most Jewish actors who co-starred alongside him, most notably Kirk Douglas, insist this was so much hogwash. They did three movies together, and if there was a nit to pick, it had to do with their opposing political views, not race or religion. Here Douglas plays David "Mickey" Marcus, Israel's first commander in 1948. Most people assume this to have been a personal project for Douglas, produced by his own Bryna Productions. What a surprise, then, to see the Batjac label as the movie begins. Wayne co–executively produced the film with Douglas to make certain the project got made. When General Randolph views the Holocaust survivors for the first time, he mutters: "God help them, 'cause that's all the help they'll get from us." Some have wrongly assumed this to be John Wayne's own dismissive attitude, but this belief, widespread in most military and political circles circa 1945, was included here to make a modern audience aware of the worldwide lack of commitment to the cause in the postwar years. Moments later Randolph allows Marcus, without authorization, to use the trucks to transport these people to safety.

THE MESSAGE: The best way to demonstrate Christian charity is to help your Jewish cousins when they're down and out.

CAPITALISM WITH A CONSCIENCE: To earn enough money so that he could produce important message movies like the pro-Zionist *Cast a Giant Shadow*, Wayne appeared in advertisements; this later one, from 1979, is for Great Western Savings.
Courtesy: © David Sutton / mptvimages.com

BIG AND BIGGER: The most rugged he-men in Hollywood shared the screen in a film that acknowledged the great similarity in appearance of top-flight tough guys Duke and Robert Mitchum. *Courtesy: mptvimages.com*

EL DORADO (1966)

Director: Howard Hawks
Screenwriter: Leigh Brackett (screenplay based on the novel *The Stars in Their Courses* by Harry Brown)
"I'm paid to risk my neck. I'll decide where and when I'll do it. This isn't it."

Gunfighter Cole Thornton rides into the small town that, along with a poem by Edgar Allan Poe, provides this film with its title. An old friend (Robert Mitchum) now serves as the local law, and Cole would prefer not to go up against the man for reasons at once professional (the fellow is his equal, perhaps better even, with a gun) and personal (an old friend is an old friend, and that means something in the World According to John Wayne). Still, Cole rides out to visit the land baron who sent him advance money. Now, though, Cole is having second thoughts, and not only because he doesn't want to tangle with a trusted buddy—something smells rotten. The small rancher Cole would put pressure on (had he accepted the land baron's offer) certainly seems a decent enough fellow. Simply put, Cole knows that to hire on for the job he's ridden so far to consider, he would end up on what he considers the wrong side, morally speaking. Perhaps most other hired guns would do that anyway, earning the term "mercenary." But—this being a John Wayne film, after all—Cole isn't one of them. So he rides off, not into the sunset, but just over the next ridge, to join the very people he was supposed to hassle, perhaps even kill.

THE MESSAGE: As Wayne's character said in The Alamo: *"There's right and there's wrong. You got to do one or the other." The ultimate measure of a man is how he chooses to act.*

THE WAR WAGON (1967)

Director: Burt Kennedy
Screenwriter: Clair Huffaker (screenplay based on Huffaker's novel *Badman*)
"Mine was taller."

Early in the tale, much of it played with a casual tongue-in-cheek aura, Wayne's Taw Jackson returns from a three-year prison stretch to a small town where he once lived as a ranch owner. Then some no-account varmint named Pierce (Bruce Cabot) framed Jackson for murder in order to seize his land. Jackson wants vengeance, hoping to steal a shipment of Pierce's gold bars. Problem is, they're being transported in an iron-plated stagecoach protected by a Gatling gun mounted on a turret, as well as a small army of mounted gunfighters. Still, Jackson figures he can manage it if he can talk Lomax (Kirk Douglas), a safecracker, to join him in this endeavor. As the two walk the dusty street, two of Pierce's gunmen block their way. Following a quick shootout, both of those would-be assassins lie dead. Lomax, hoping to play a little bit of one-upmanship on his former enemy turned uneasy ally, smiles and brags: "Mine hit the ground first." Without even a moment's hesitation, Jackson tosses back the above quote. Both Wayne and Douglas had become genre icons, each moving into maturity (a nice term for "old age") with dignity. However great both were, only one Mr. Machismo could rule the roost. As Jackson shuffles off following that repartee, Lomax's forlorn face leaves no doubt as to who that is.

THE MESSAGE: Always get in the final word. Part of being a winner has less to do with what happens than with how it's perceived. Verbally seize control of the narrative, and you'll always come out on top.

THE GRAND OL' MAN: While shooting *The War Wagon* with frequent co-star Kirk Douglas, Wayne took time out to pose with popular television cowboy stars Clint Walker, David Carradine, Michael Ansara, Hugh O'Brian, Chuck Connors, and Clayton Moore. *Courtesy: © Gunther / mptvimages.com*

HELLFIGHTERS (1968)

Director: Andrew V. McLaglen
Screenwriter: Clair Huffaker
"This was bound to happen sooner or later, and each time I'll go."

This one-of-a-kind film, inspired by the life of Red Adair (who served as technical advisor), lionizes a group of unique professionals: the elite firefighters, based in Houston, Texas, who fly all over the world to end oil well fires. If they appear to casual observers like cowboys, the opposite is true: The first thing Chance Buckman (Duke) does upon arrival is to determine the risk factors involved in fighting a fire. If it's likely to claim the life of a team member, he refuses to become involved. In most cases Chance analyzes the problem intellectually, devising a specific way to approach and attack the current fire, since no two are the same to the trained eye. Then, with the primary commitment always to the safety of each man, he will cautiously go about neutralizing the situation. Years earlier Chance's San Francisco high society wife (Vera Miles) left him, not because her love for the man had diminished, rather as her anxiety grew more extreme each time he left on a job. They are reunited when he accepts an executive position with an oil company. Then their son-in-law (Jim Hutton), who now oversees the Hellfighters, takes on an assignment in a Latin American country that no one but Chance could handle. His decision is a foregone conclusion.

THE MESSAGE: A man's gotta do what a man's gotta do; his woman must either accept and live with that or cut and run.

THE GREEN BERETS (1968)

Directors: Ray Kellogg and John Wayne
Screenwriter: James Lee Barrett (screenplay based on a novel of the same name by Robin Moore)
"You're what this 'thing' is all about!"

As Col. Mike Kirby, Wayne says that to a South Vietnamese boy at the film's conclusion. Kirby serves as the Duke's spokesman in his most personal project since *The Alamo*. The undeclared Vietnam War, unlike World War II, did not convince most Americans we were involved in a crusade against evil. Confusion was the order of the day. Norman Mailer's novel *Why Are We in Vietnam?* ends with one ordinary guy asking that of a friend. "Damned if I know!" came the reply. Wayne decided in 1965 to make a movie that would offer his own answer to that question. Although many in the press attacked *The Green Berets* as being a pro-war film, both this and every one of Duke's World War II projects were anti-war. If he was "pro" anything, it was in support of the men and women who risk their lives fighting for what they believe to be right. As in *The Alamo*, this film's "small band of soldiers" is multiethnic in makeup, including an African American (Raymond St. Jacques) and Asians (Jack Soo, Irene Tsu).

Audiences are shown the Russian and Chinese weaponry that the North Vietnamese were being supplied with, along with troops. Wayne's thesis: Once the Soviet bloc made the first move, then the United States had an obligation to likewise get involved.

THE MESSAGE: The only way the United States could profess belief in everyone's right to self-determination and still hold its head high was to offer a counterforce to the international communists attempting to deny the people of South Vietnam a choice between communism and democracy.

THE LAST WARRIOR: Compared to World War II-era movies, few films were made to propagandize what had become a controversial involvement for the US; Wayne rose to the occasion by producing his own movie on Vietnam. *Courtesy: mptvimages.com*

TRUE GRIT (1969)

Director: Henry Hathaway
Screenwriter: Marguerite Roberts (screenplay based on a novel of the same name by Charles Portis)

"Well, come and see a fat old man some time!"

Many aficionados of Wayne (in his Oscar-winning role) may prefer a more often quoted line. As Rooster Cogburn (Duke) and the evil Ned Pepper (Robert Duvall) make ready to shoot it out on horseback, like knights of old riding to a joust, the tired old hero shouts: "Fill your hands, you son of a bitch!" Rooster, of course, is referring to guns. As hard as it might be to believe today, the final word of that phrase caused some concern way back when, considering that this was a family film. However appealing that scene may be, sentimentalists prefer Rooster's final farewell to young Mattie Ross (Kim Darby) moments before Wayne (actually, a stuntman) jumps his horse over a fence and rides off into the sunset. Here is Wayne making the Rooster role his own. In Portis's novel, Cogburn is forty-something; Wayne, at sixty-one, reimagined the one-eyed marshal even as the persona that had defined traditional masculinity, American-style, openly admitted that twilight time was nigh. Incidentally, anyone who believes Wayne was the fiercest opponent of allowing once blacklisted writers (owing to Red leanings in the 1950s) to work again ought to consider that he okayed Roberts, thought to be a communist, for this project. With Wayne it was all about the work: He loved the way she wrote and had no qualms at all about having this liberal lady author work on one of his projects.

THE MESSAGE: The key to growin' old with dignity is to accept that as a fact and maintain a sense of humor about the situation.

AT LONG LAST OSCAR: The statuette that Duke deserved for *Red River*, *Sands of Iwo Jima*, *The Quiet Man*, *She Wore a Yellow Ribbon* or *The Searchers* was finally awarded to him for *True Grit*, more as an acknowledgment of career achievement than for this particular performance. Here he is pictured with Kim Darby.   *Courtesy: mptvimages.com*

THE UNDEFEATED (1969)

Director: Andrew V. McLaglen
Screenwriters: James Lee Barrett and Stanley Hough
"We're all Americans."

As Union officer Col. John Henry Thomas, the Duke says this to a Confederate commander (Royal Dano) after being forced by rebels into a bloody battle days after the was officially ended. Despising violence, Thomas is upset and stunned to learn that the rebs did indeed know about the Confederate army's surrender at Appomattox. Why then did they refuse to set down their arms, and thus avoid unnecessary bloodshed? Because, simply put, Thomas's men were invaders on Southern soil. Thomas can't help but admire that deep sense of pride in hailing from a particular region. All the same, there's a larger issue at hand here, as quoted above.

Though set in the post–Civil War era, *The Undefeated* serves as a metaphor for America in 1969. The country was nastily divided on many issues, civil rights being one of the most significant. Many in the South resented the federal government's intrusion into what they considered their concerns about white/black relations. Here then is John Wayne's statement as to the absolute need to heal. Later he and his Northern cowboys, with difficulty, get to know another group of rebels. Wayne and their leader (Rock Hudson) set differences aside and become friends. Thomas even teaches the initially resistant Southerners integration, insisting that his adopted Indian son (Roman Gabriel) be allowed to date a pretty young Southern girl.

THE MESSAGE: As Wayne's on-screen incarnation of historical John Chisum will put it in Duke's next Western: Change is usually for the good.

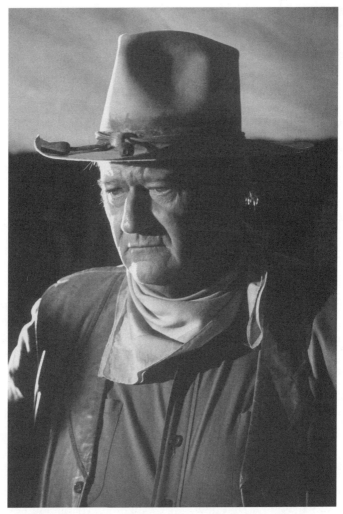

A FACE WORTHY OF MT. RUSHMORE: By the time Wayne returned to his standby role as head of a cattle drive in *The Undefeated* and *The Cowboys* (seen here), he had aged gracefully into a monumental American figurehead. *Courtesy: © David Sutton / mptvimages.com*

CHISUM (1970)

Director: Andrew V. McLaglen
Screenwriter: Andrew J. Fenady
"No matter where people go, sooner or later there's the law. And sooner or later they find God's already been there!"

Chisum is one of those big-scale Westerns specifically designed and written for John Wayne as the last great surviving star of old-fashioned oaters. Duke plays John Chisum, the real-life New Mexico ranch owner who in 1878 found himself in a range war with longtime enemies, hiring drifter Pat Garrett and young Billy the Kid first as ranch hands, and then as guns.

Wayne utters the above quotation when his fictional foreman, Mr. Pepper (Ben Johnson), considers the violence and sighs: "You know, there's an old saying . . . there's no law west of Dodge and no God west of the Pecos." Wayne considers his trusted friend (and dramatic foil) before answering: "Wrong!" He then goes on to speak his most significant lines in the film.

Here is a case, as in so many of the later films Duke chose to make, in which the character speaks not for himself but the actor playing him. No matter how set and unchangeable things seem on the surface at the present moment, life around us is constantly changing. And as Wayne makes clear in this film, he sees change not in a reactionary but in a progressive way: "Well, usually change is for the best."

THE MESSAGE: However barren and godforsaken any territory may seem, that's an illusion. There's a greater force at work in the universe. At difficult times it may appear to be gone, but in God's good time it will return.

HISTORY VS. HOLLYWOOD: The real John Chisum was a quiet businessman, never involved in gunplay; for a John Wayne movie, his involvement in the Lincoln County War had to be jazzed up considerably. *Courtesy: © David Sutton / mptvimages.com*

RIO LOBO (1970)

Director: Howard Hawks
Screenwriters: Burton Wohl and Leigh Brackett
"I've been called many things, but not 'comfortable.'"

During the Civil War, Union cavalry commander Col. Cord McNally and his men are caught in a Confederate trap. Among the dead is a young officer who had become a foster son to McNally. When the war ends, he sets out to track down the man responsible. His target is not the rebel soldier who fired the fatal shot, but the traitor in his own ranks who sold out him out, acting solely for mercenary gain. However much Wayne believed in capitalism, there's a difference between the enlightened form of that system and raw capitalism at its worst—devoid of human values. Even as justice must be tempered by mercy, so in the World According to John Wayne must the free market system be underscored by morality.

The final film to be directed by Howard Hawks contains a passel of his strong females ("the Hawksian woman," film historian Robin Wood once tagged them), their characters and dialogue written by Leigh Brackett, a well-known tough-lady screenwriter. One of her final Hollywood assignments was to develop Princess Leia for George Lucas's *Star Wars*. Back in *Red River* or even *Rio Bravo*, such ladies were romantically paired with the Duke. Now they still adore him but in a fatherly (dare we say grandfatherly?) way, one going so far as to claim that she feels completely "comfortable" with him while camping at night on the prairie.

THE MESSAGE: We all have our seasons in the sun, and it's no shame to move into late autumn as far as the ladies are concerned. That's what the term "aging gracefully" is all about.

THE LAST BUGLE: Those Civil War cavalry officers Wayne often embodied were revisited in Howard Hawks's tale of a man whose mission does not end when the final Taps is sounded but who continues the good fight. *Courtesy: © David Sutton / mptvimages.com*

BIG JAKE (1971)

Director: George Sherman
Screenwriters: Harry Julian Fink and Rita M. Fink
"There's two reasons to kill: survival and meat."

Following the release of Sam Peckinpah's *Wild Bunch*, Hollywood found it ever more difficult to amass financing for Westerns about the frontier's golden age. Even John Wayne necessarily shifted over to a twentieth-century setting. Here Duke plays Jacob McCandles, an anachronistic figure whose grandson has been kidnapped. Since everyone else (Jake's sons included) has become too civilized for their own good, he heads up one last old-time posse to bring the varmints to justice and return the eight-year-old in one piece. Not surprisingly, things work out just fine—after a whole lot of bloodletting.

For those who believed Wayne's era as a box office attraction was over, Big Jake disproved that. Back in the mid-1960s, his huge hits like *El Dorado* and *The War Wagon* brought in a hefty $6 million apiece on investments of approximately $2 million per. In the post–*Easy Rider* (1969) movie world, supposedly old-fashioned Westerns had bitten the dust. Yet *Big Jake* scored more than a whopping $7.5 million. Some attribute this to a conservative backlash against the new cinema then evolving. Folks who were nostalgic for the old Hollywood lined up to see the Duke to relive a little bit of the good ol' days.

THE MESSAGE: The biblical adage "an eye for an eye, a tooth for a tooth" was not a cry for extreme punishment, but the opposite. Anyone who commits a minor mishap ought to have justice tempered by mercy. However, any man who threatens your own right to live ought to be dealt with swiftly. And of course, one has to eat.

STILL TALL IN THE SADDLE: Though the years were catching up with him, Wayne could still embody the old lawman who tracks down the meanest men in the West and, like a good Mountie, always gets his man. *Courtesy: © David Sutton / mptvimages.com*

THE COWBOYS (1972)

Director: Mark Rydell
Screenwriters: Irving Ravetch, Harriet Frank Jr., and William Dale Jennings (screenplay based on a novel of the same name by Jennings)
"I don't hold jail against you, but I hate a liar."

Texas rancher Wil Andersen finds himself between a rock and a hard place. It's time for a long drive, but his regular drovers have all run off in search of gold. Then several drifters, led by a grinning giant (Bruce Dern), ride up and ask for work. Wayne's character gets a bad feeling in his gut and quickly catches them in a lie. Obviously they've been behind bars rather than cowboying. Duke dismisses them in favor of some inexperienced but honest kids. When Dern's rawhider asks if he and his boys might deserve a second chance, Andersen makes clear he absolutely would have hired these boys if only they'd told the truth.

Here is one of the few post-*Alamo* Wayne Westerns that was not designed specifically for Wayne by a team dedicated to enshrining that growing American legend. The screenwriters are best known for liberal-social collaborations, and the director expressed shock and even, as a lefty, outrage that the conservative Wayne wanted to meet with him and humbly request the role. Then again, Wayne's politics were never as simplistic as those who chose to demonize him believed. Wayne found himself attracted to one of the first films to come out in favor of diversity: The "boys" include Spanish and Jewish volunteers, and the cook (Roscoe Lee Browne) is an African American.

THE MESSAGE: Religion, ethnicity, and gender mean nothing compared to the worth of the person inside, as expressed in deed and word.

STUDYING WITH THE MASTER: All the boys who began this fateful cattle drive in *The Cowboys* only to become young men in the process could rightly claim: "Everything I need to know, I learned from John Wayne." *Courtesy: mptvimages.com*

THE TRAIN ROBBERS (1973)

Director and screenwriter: Burt Kennedy
"What a gun rides anywhere for? Money! The more of it, the more chances you take."

Wayne's character, Lane, offers this seemingly cynical assessment in one of the oddest of the Duke's later vehicles: a rare occasion when the aging Wayne played not a cattle/land baron—so appropriate to the star's status as king of old-fashioned Westerns—but rather a throwback to his earlier loner character. *Hondo*, of course, was the greatest of all such films. It hardly seems coincidental that the character we meet here shares that hombre's last name. Or that the woman (Ann-Margret) who offers Lane a chance to make a financial killing fast is Mrs. Lowe, the name of Geraldine Page's female lead in that beloved 1953 Batjac production.

Lane has been hired to round up a group of scoundrels (one more and they'd be seven, though far from magnificent) to help the dubious lady locate money that her late husband stole from a train, then return it to the proper authorities—or so she claims. *The Train Robbers* is minor stuff compared to most of Wayne's large-budget 1970s projects, reminiscent in scope and size of Republic Pictures' way of making movies back in the 1940s. One unpleasant group member (Rod Taylor) is something akin to a last frontier Frankenstein's monster cobbled together from bits and pieces of old Forrest Tucker roles. The experience is like watching a B movie script shot with an A+ cast, its slight story line rounded out a by strong production values and a spirited playing of overly familiar scenes.

THE MESSAGE: A true professional knows that the more you stand to make, the greater risk you assume.

ONCE A MAVERICK, ALWAYS A MAVERICK: After playing a string of
respectable cattle barons, the Duke returned one final time to the type
of gun-for-hire characters in *The Train Robbers* he'd early on made
famous. *Courtesy: © David Sutton / mptvimages.com*

CAHILL U.S. MARSHAL (1973)

Director: Andrew V. McLaglen
Screenwriters: Harry Julien Fink and Rita M. Fink
"Mister, I ain't got a bigoted bone in my body. You don't drop that axe, I'll blast you to hell as quick as I would a white man."

J.D. Cahill (Duke) has a problem. While he's been out rounding up outlaws, his own boys (Gary Grimes and Clay O'Brien) have grown so desperate for attention that they join up with a notorious outlaw (George Kennedy). There's a generation gap theme there, and not entirely flattering to older folks. If only parents would spend less time at work and pay more attention to their children, perhaps those kids wouldn't be so rebellious. More essential to this minor, routine item was a desire to set the record straight. In May 1971 Wayne had been lassoed into sounding insensitive about the civil rights issue in a *Playboy* interview. He came out against any "entitlements," true, though race had nothing to do with it. Wayne believed in the American work ethic, which encourages people to take pride in their work. And Duke's version of the often told Alamo story was the first to reveal that the heroes of the day included African Americans, Spanish and Mexican Americans, and women. You might say Wayne was into diversity long before that concept became co-opted by the left (although it's actually an all-American and apolitical point-of-view). Wayne's dissatisfaction with the welfare system had to do with those who cheated to beat the system, and more of those people were white than black. He despised all such cheaters equally.

THE MESSAGE: Bigotry is just plain stupid. If you threaten someone's life, expect to be paid back in kind, regardless of your skin color.

McQ (1974)

Director: John Sturges
Screenwriter: Lawrence Roman
"There's a bar over there. Let's get a drink."

"I'm up to my butt in gas!" McQ (Duke) exclaims when his car is smashed from two sides by trucks driven by men out to kill him. Fans of the star and this film (the first, and better, of two contemporary cop films Wayne agreed to star in after turning down *Dirty Harry*) cite that as their favorite line in the film. However, more profound are the final words McQ says. Early on, word reaches police officer McQ that his former partner on the force has been murdered. McQ sets out on a vengeance trail, initially blaming Santiago (Al Lettieri), the local Mr. Big drug dealer. Then (and this comes as a surprise from Wayne, who ordinarily appeared only in films complimentary to men of any risky profession) he learns that not only was his pal on the take, but so are an incredible number of other policemen. Having handed in his badge, McQ brings the guilty parties to justice. Unlike Clint Eastwood in the final scene of *Dirty Harry*, throwing his badge away as if he's lost faith in the system, Wayne says the above to the chief (Eddie Albert) and one honest cop (James Watkins) when they request he rejoin the good fight. Here is the difference between Wayne and Eastwood, and a hint as to why Duke said yes to this film.

THE MESSAGE: Sometimes you'll need a stiff drink to do it, but one way or another, get back into the good fight. And do it within the system, not as a self-appointed vigilante.

ROOSTER COGBURN (1975)

Director: Stuart Millar
Screenwriters: Charles Portis and Martha Hyer (under the pen name "Martin Julien")
"I'll be damned if she didn't get the last word in again."

The title character states this at the end of Duke's third-from-last film and penultimate Western. Here Katharine Hepburn as Eula Goodnight, daughter of a deceased preacher, once again does what she has throughout the film: prove in action as well as words that a strong woman is the equal of any man. Wayne as Rooster gets the message—and a perfect one it is for a film released during the height of the feminist movement. Complaints about Duke's giving Maureen O'Hara a good spanking to put her in her place a dozen years earlier in *McLintock!* were countered and muted by this overdue recognition of a female's worth. In fact, though, check back over *Hondo* and most of the other films in the John Wayne canon, and you'll discover one remarkable woman after another, each treated with the respect due her. It's worth noting that Katharine Hepburn had originally been slated to star opposite the Duke in that film. Most people suspect that the reason she passed on that role was the vast political divide in the 1950s, largely over the Hollywood blacklist that Wayne supported and she detested. This was the final film of producer Hal B. Wallis, who had overseen *The Maltese Falcon, Yankee Doodle Dandy, Becket,* and several Elvis Presley musicals.

THE MESSAGE: Any man worth his own salt will stand back and gladly let any formidable woman get in the final word.

WHEN ROOSTER COGBURN MET A LADY: Wayne told the press that he guessed Spencer Tracy, Clark Gable, and Humphrey Bogart were all gazing down from that great Tinseltown in the sky, envying his own belated co-star gig with Katharine Hepburn.
Courtesy: © David Sutton / mptvimages.com

BRANNIGAN (1975)

Director: Douglas Hickox
Screenwriters: Christopher Trumbo, Michael Butler, William P. McGivern, and William W. Norton
"Knock, knock!"

The Duke turned down the role of Dirty Harry because he didn't approve of or agree with Detective Callahan's extreme vigilantism, which included killing a serial-murder suspect rather than bringing the man in for trial. The John Wayne hero plays by the rules, even if he has to bend them from time to time in order to get the job done. Here again Wayne was the perfect realist, rejecting extremes of idealism and cynicism. One early sequence in this contemporary cop film reveals just such an approach in action. In Chicago Brannigan knows he needs to apprehend a minor crook before that sleazebag can dispose of the evidence. So he kicks open the door, catching the bad guy in the act. After Brannigan is inside, he utters the above line, as he will later do when going after a far more dangerous Mr. Big type (John Vernon) in London. Brannigan even threatens to blow the little rat away if he doesn't provide some important information. But here's the difference between Wayne's persona and that of Eastwood: The Duke's gun is not loaded. And he would not shoot an unarmed man, no matter what, not even in this soiled modern world.

THE MESSAGE: Sometimes it's necessary to play fast and loose with the rules, because no system is perfect. But there are limits beyond which we ought not to go if we believe in the idea of civilization. Use your heart and your mind in negotiating that thin line! And always respect human life, even with those who barely rate as human.

THE SHOOTIST (1976)

Director: Don Siegel
Screenwriters: Glendon Swarthout, Miles Hood Swarthout, and Scott Hale (screenplay based on a novel of the same name by Glendon Swarthout)

"I won't be wronged. I won't be insulted. I won't be laid a hand on. I don't do those things to other people, and I require the same from them."

John Wayne battled cancer for over a decade and at times it seemed as if the Duke might even lick this antagonist. But the big guy knew it was only a matter of time when he agreed to star in this, his swan song. John B. Books is an aging gunfighter who knows he won't survive long after a doctor (James Stewart) informs him of an inoperable growth. Rather than slowly waste away, Books decides to go down fighting against an old enemy (Richard Boone) or a new one (Hugh O'Brian). First, though, he wins the heart of a lonely widow (Lauren Bacall) and her impressionable, idol-worshipping son (Ron Howard).

In the opening scenes Howard in a voice-over sums up Books's career. To depict the young John Books, director Siegel employed clips from earlier Wayne movies, showing the star in various stages of his life. This apotheosis of everything Wayne ever did and said on-screen was his last opportunity to both demonstrate his values through action and state them outright. He does precisely that in the monologue cited above. Here is rugged individualism at its most poignant and self-sufficient.

THE MESSAGE: Do unto others as you would have them do unto you? Sure. But make damn well certain they understand that the deal starts with them and that their individuality will be respected just so long as everyone grasps that life is a two-way street.

THE LAST SUNSET: As John W. Books, an old gunslinger facing the one adversary he could not defeat (cancer), John Wayne found his perfect final role, teaming him with Lauren Bacall. *Courtesy: © David Sutton / mptvimages.com*

INDEX

Moore, Dennis, 29
Moore, Robin, 139
morality, 53, 62, 94, 135, 147, 159
Morgan, George, 2
Morgan, Harry, 121
movie realism *vs.* fantasy, 80
Mulhall, Jack, *10*, 11

Nakamura, Henry, 92
Native Americans, 6, 21, 35, 53, 65, 95, 124
Natteford, Jack Francis, 12
Natwick, Mildred, 67
Negulesco, Jean, 129
New Frontier, The, 28
Nichols, Dudley, 33
Nolan, Lloyd, 127
"no pain, no gain," 1
North to Alaska, 113–14
Norton, William W., 159
Nosler, Lloyd, 29
nuclear weapon testing sites, as filming locations, 97
Nugent, Frank S., 65, 67, 75, 83, 95, 126

O'Brian, Hugh, 128, *137*, 160
O'Brien, Clay, 155
O'Hara, Maureen, 77, 83, *84*, 157
O'Keefe, Dennis, 55
Olson, Nancy, 82
O'Neill, Eugene, 36
Operation Pacific, 80, *81*
Ornitz, Samuel, 39
Oursler, Fulton, 129
Owen, George, 48
Ozarks, 44

Page, Geraldine, 87, *88*
Paradise Canyon, 23, *24*
Paramount, 30
Parrish, Helen, 45
Parsons, Lindsley, 15, 23, 27
patrol torpedo (PT) boat squadrons, 57

Peabody, Jack, 1
Perry, Matthew, 106
Pidgeon, Walter, 41
Pierce, Franklin, 106
Pierson, Carl, 23
"Pilgrim," 124
Pittsburgh, 48
Portis, Charles, 141, 157
Postal, Florence, 1
Poverty Row, 6, 15, 19
Powell, Dick, 97
Preminger, Otto, 128
Presnell, Robert, Jr., 102
progress, 2, 6
promise-keeping, 19, 41, 65, 115, 151
punishment, crime-fitting, 67, 149
Purcell, Gertrude, 45

Quantrill, William Clark, 41
Quiet Man, The, *63*, 83, *84*
Quinn, Anthony, 61
quitting, 1

racism, 95, 143, 155
Rackin, Martin, 107, 113
railroad industry, 59
railway industry, 2
Rainbow Valley, 26
Raines, Ella, 56
Raintree County, 121
Ralston, Vera, 59, 71, *72*
Ravetch, Irving, 151
Ray, Nicholas, 79, 127
Reap the Wild Wind, 40
reciprocity, 42
redemption, 30, 89, 99
Red River, 62, 69, 70
"Red Sails in the Sunset" (song), 36
Red Scare, 82, 141
Reed, Tom, 47, 48
regulations, 55
relationship advice, 12, 27, 33, 68, 82, 83, 138

Taylor, Don, 79
Taylor, Eric, 82
Taylor, Rod, 153
teamwork, 86, 123
Telegraph Trail, The, 6, 7
Terhune, Max, 31, *32*
Texas Terror, 25
They Were Expendable, 57, 101
Three Faces West, 39
3 Godfathers, 67
Three Mesquiteers, 31
Three Musketeers, The, *10*, 11, 17
Three Texas Steers, 31, *32*
thrillers, 2, 5
Tiomkin, Dimitri, 111
Tombstone, 23
Track of the Cat (production), 91
tradition, 2, 6
Train Robbers, The, 153, *154*
Travers, Barry, 49
Trevor, Claire, 33, 41
Trouble Along the Way, 85
True Grit, 141, *142*
Trumbo, Christopher, 159
truth, 25, 71, 117
Tsu, Irene, 139
Tugend, Harry, 38
20th Century Fox, 119
Twist, John, 48, 62, 94
Tycoon, 62, 63

Undefeated, The, 143, 144

Van Cleef, Lee, *118*
vengeance, 15, 44, 68, 99, 100, 136, 156
Vernon, John, 159
victimization, 59
Vietnam War, 139, *140*
vigilantism, 156, 159
Vitagraph Pictures, 6
Vorhaus, Bernard, 39
vulnerability, 29

Waggner, George, 71, 80
Wake of the Red Witch, 68
Walker, Clint, *137*
Wallace, Richard, 62
Wallis, Hal B., 157
Walsh, Maurice, 83
Walsh, Raoul, 1, 41
Walthall, Henry B., 8
war, 107, 139
war movies. *See also* World War II movies
    Battle of the Alamo, 111
    cavalry-themed, 17, 75, 77
    Civil War, 107, 121, 143, 147
    Vietnam War, 139
Warner Bros., 6, 14
War of the Wildcats, 53
War Wagon, The, 136, 149
Watkins, James, 156
Wayne, Aissa, *90*, *125*
Wayne, Ethan, *51*
Wayne, John. *See also related topics and
        movie titles*
    children of, *51*, *90*
    directorial roles, 111, *112*, 115,
        116, 139
    in football uniform, 37
    with Ford, *58*
    at home, *104*
    horseback riding skills, 28
    life philosophies, 111
    miscasting of, 97
    movie character complexity, 46
    movie character personae and
        symbolism, 20, *108*
    movies written for, 87, 124
    politics and, 87, 92, 111, 151, 157
    production roles, 64, 71, 87, 91, 99,
        132, 133
    on set, *108*
    with television cowboys, *137*
    wives of, *90*
    yachts of, *51*
Wayne, Patrick, *78*

ABOUT THE AUTHOR

DOUGLAS BRODE is a screenwriter, playwright, novelist, graphic novelist, film historian, and multi-award-winning journalist. Born and raised on Long Island, he traveled upstate to attend SUNY Geneseo as an undergrad in 1961. After completing graduate work in Shakespearean studies and creative writing at Syracuse University, he and his wife Sue (Johnson) remained in central New York and raised a family. Brode became a film critic for such local newspapers as the *Syracuse New Times* and *Post-Standard*, as well as daily commentator on WHEN-AM radio and a member of the TV news teams for the local ABC and CBS affiliates. While teaching at Onondaga Community College, Brode created the first approved cinema studies program at any two-year college in the State University of New York system. He then joined the faculty of Syracuse University, the Newhouse School of Public Communications, Department of TV, Film, and Digital Media. Brode wrote the screenplay for the motion picture *Midnight Blue* (1996) starring Harry Dean Stanton and Dean Stockwell, as well as the novels *Sweet Prince: The Passion of Hamlet* (2004) and *"PATSY!": The Life and Times of Lee Harvey Oswald* (2013). The author of over forty books on movies and the mass media, his work includes *Films of the Fifties*, *Films of Steven Spielberg*, *Denzel Washington* (a biography), *Shakespeare in the Movies* (for Oxford University Press), two books on Walt Disney—*From Walt to Woodstock* (2004) and *Multiculturalism and the Mouse* (2006)—and *Elvis Cinema and Popular Culture* (2007) for McFarland Press. He and Carol (widow of Rod) Serling collaborated on *Rod Serling and "The Twilight Zone": The Official 50th Anniversary Tribute* (2009). Brode brought Texas history to life in the graphic novel *Yellow Rose of Texas: The Myth of Emily*

Morgan (2010), illustrated by Joe Orsak. Brode's books on Westerns include *Shooting Stars of the Small Screen: An Encyclopedia of TV Western Actors* (2009) and *Dream West: Politics and Religion in Cowboy Movies* (2013), both for University of Texas Press, Austin. He appears regularly as a guest on such national TV and radio broadcasts as *The Dennis Miller Show*. Brode contributes articles to *American Cowboy*'s annual John Wayne tribute issue as well as other features for that magazine, and has written for *True West* and *Wild West*, as well as *TV Guide* and *Rolling Stone*. Currently, he and his wife reside in San Antonio, where (when not writing) Brode teaches at the University of Texas, Department of Philosophy, Humanities & Classics.

AT THE ALAMO: The author visits the set of John Wayne's most personal film. *Courtesy: Shane Brode*